AF821947

Queen Moves

7 Steps To Soar In Your Finances

Affirm And Pursue 2021 by Yvonne Brown
All Rights Reserved.
Printed in the United States of America.
For information, address Affirm And Pursue,
PA

Affirm And Pursue
www.affirmandpursueacademy.com

Designed by Maximum Evolution

The Library Of Congress Catalog in Publication Data
Is available upon request.

Manuscript Edited and Formatted by Maximum Evolution

ISBN 978-1-7349735-8-7

All Rights Reserved worldwide. No part of this publication may be reproduced, distributed, or transmitted in any form or by any means, including photocopying, recording scanning or other electronic or mechanical methods, without the prior written permission of the publisher or author, Yvonne Brown, except in the case of brief quotations embodied in critical reviews and certain other noncommercial use permitted by copyright law. Please do not participate in or encourage piracy of copyrighted materials which are in violation of author's rights. For more information on purchases in bulk for promotional, educational, business use, or speaking events, please contact Yvonne Brown @ yvonnebrowncoaching@gmail.com.

Disclaimer

This publication is designed to provide accurate and reliable information in regard to the subject matter covered. It is sold with the understanding that the author is not engaged in rendering legal, financial, accounting or professional services. Laws vary from state-to-state and if you require legal advice, financial advice or expert assistance, you should seek the services of a professional. The author disclaims any liability that is incurred from the use or application of the contents of this book.

While the author has made every effort to provide accurate references and internet address at the time of publication, neither the publisher nor the author assumes any responsibility for errors, or changes that occur after publication.

Dedicated to my father, Lloyd Brown, whose memories of hard work and sacrifice for his family's future will forever fuel me to serve with purity and with God's leading.

To my family, who keeps me grounded and constantly listens to my ideas and provides continuous support to me even at ground zero. Together we will continue to plant seeds to change our children's financial future.

Align yourself with those who have a kingdom mindset.

A *Kingdom Mindset Wins Every Time - Yvonne Brown*

Acknowledgments

Cortea Bess

Jeanette Brown

jeanettembrown@gmail.com

Danielle Batiste

dmbatiste@yahoo.com,

Diabetes Made Better LLC

Rashida Roberts

targetfinancialcoach@gmail.com,

Target Financial,

www.cashflowconvo.com @targetfinancial

Robin Durwin Libby

Beauty By Robin Studios, beautybyrobinstudios@gmail.com,

https://www.beautybyrobinstudios.com,

@beauty_by_robin_studios

Duania Hall

dkhallfirst@gmail.com, www.duaniahall.com,

@dh_motivating4life

Dr. Tamara Hill- Bennett

Sustain Your Biz 2 Win, www.sustainyourbiz2win.org,

@2020eyedr

Tiffany Alexander

From Broken To Beautiful, FBTBLLC.com,

@Brokentobeautifulboutique

Dawn Brown

daybreakdb@gmail.com, Daybreak Graphics, @daybreakgraphics

Nancy Fleurancois

nancyfluer@yahoo.com

For additional complimentary bonuses: Download your monthly budget workbook at https://yvonnebrown.podia.com/affirmpursue-bonus. Use Coupon Code: FREE

SUBMIT A 5-STAR REVIEW

Please feel free to snap a picture with a copy of the book and leave a review at reviews.yvonnebrownexhales.com.

Table of Contents

Introduction

Who is a Queen?

What is a Queen Move?

Affirm and pursue your crown by reframing your mindset and learning effective tools you can use to create sustainable financial health and wealth. Turn your financial woes into achievable financial goals. You may have heard the saying, *"If you don't know where you're going, any road will get you there."* The same can be said of becoming a queen... If you don't know who you are, then you cannot establish your Kingdom; therefore, forfeiting your crown. You need a kingdom mindset to establish a financial Kingdom. You need to think like a Queen to become a queen.

You may be wondering if it is your time. You may have asked yourself the following questions: *Do I need to have a goal to start saving money? Is saving money for something I desire that effective? Is a debt-free ticket possible? How is the habit of saving money going to benefit me? Will budgeting help me fulfill my goals?*

These questions usually arise during the start of the New Year, or during a financial reset. Having an achievable goal is good because it allows you to celebrate your WINS when you meet each goal. Especially when you have the right mindset and an accountability partner or coach who pushes you and while offering positive reinforcement. The feeling of accomplishing a financial goal is incredible, but if it is not S.M.A.R.T.: Specific, Measurable, Achievable, Relevant, and Time-Based, it will more than likely not yield the desired outcome, and that my Queen will only build frustration or a feeling of self-defeat.

Queen, it's time to stop dwelling in defeat, change your mindset, and establish your financial foundation. If you are a woman between the ages of

25-55 who knows that you are not living in the financial freedom or success you imagined, then this book is for you. Queen, it is time to maximize this opportunity and use the golden nuggets in this book to build your solid financial foundation and establish your Queendom. There is no time like the present.

Are you ready?

Do you believe it's possible?

Can you claim it?

Let's go!

Chapter 1: Get Out of the Rut--The First Step, Reset!

A Queen's Nugget Of Wisdom-

> *Your thoughts shape your vision. You see what you choose to see. - Anonymous*

The first step in achieving financial health and wealth is changing how you think about and define personal success. First, you must adopt a Queen mindset. You may be asking yourself who is a Queen? And what is the Queen's mindset? How does this relate to building financial health and wealth?

There are many definitions of the word Queen. Remember in chess, the Queen is the most powerful figure. In this context, the definition of a Queen describes women who are uplifting, empowering, and loving; we are the women who dare to face life's curveballs and debt with perseverance, determination, and ambition. Queens affirm and pursue their goals with tenacity until they succeed. I was not always a Queen, but I decided to change how I thought about and approached life, finances, and debt. We get to choose who we are in this world. Knowing you get to choose is a powerful tool to help you shift into the crown you were born to wear.

It's a painful place when you have an enormous amount of debt and are unable to see the light at the end of the tunnel. Queen, I know all too well how that feels; I carried a great deal of debt when I was unemployed for 14 months. It was one of the most difficult seasons of my life. Throughout that season, I had many negative automatic thoughts about myself, my decisions, and my abilities. Trust me when I say, you wish you never had any debt when you have no consistent income coming in to pay your lenders timely. All the choices I made up to that point, I know it was because I was operating in an unhealthy state, a poverty mindset. Subsequently, although I yearned for a job to pay my bills, if I didn't make a conscious decision to change my mindset, nothing would keep me from making unhealthy money decisions. Operating under a poverty mindset results in negative automatic thoughts or what some refer to as "Stinking Thinking." Some of the negative thoughts I had were:

I'll never recover financially.

I can't believe I ruined my credit score.

Yvonne, you have two degrees. How did you end up here?

So much for that strategy track for my retirement goal.

No one will pay me what I deserve when I get a job because I've been without one for so long.

What are some of the automatic thoughts you have had about yourself when facing debt or a financial curveball? Write 5 of them down below:

1.

2.

3.

4.

5.

As a Queen, change is paramount to how you move forward with grace. Therefore, it is important to counteract those negative thoughts with positive thinking. What are some positive thoughts that you should say? Write 5 of them below:

1.

2.

3.

4.

5.

Queen, you must change your perspective if you want to establish your Queendom. *Assessing your current impoverished perspective and making a choice to adopt a Queen mindset is the first and foundational Queen Move.* To do this, one must replace old negative thoughts with new self-affirming thoughts. This is the beginning of wisdom, to reclaim your thoughts and rework how you speak about and to yourself. So now let's talk about some other nuggets of wisdom to adopt that can help reshape your mindset in your financial journey towards affirming and pursuing your goal of financial health and wealth.

> ***Remember: Financial education is a lifetime commitment. Money Management is 80% behavior and 20% logic.***

I will repeat this statement throughout this book because I want you to grab hold of this fact!

Financial literacy must continue throughout your lifetime, simply because the more you discover, the more you find out that you need to learn. Most people never take the time to educate themselves. They are ok with accepting the status quo. They go to work, get their check, balance their accounts, and that's it. They take what an advisor says as the gospel and never truly educate themselves or stay abreast of nuances within the financial realm, and then wonder why they have financial problems that can't just be solved with more money. The solution is not more money, but rather changing your behavioral responses to how you handle money. It requires changing your relationship to money. You may have heard the adage: ***money is a good tool but a cruel master.***

The Financial Landscape: Attacking The Debt Problem From The Root

We are surrounded by debt every day. We are living in an economy that profits from consumers who make bad money decisions. However, this doesn't have to be your story; based on one's values, beliefs, and relationship with money, it can be seen as a good thing and not necessarily bad. The fact is the debt toll has taken on the masses, especially with women, isn't something to dismiss lightly. *According to a 2018 report by the American Association of University Women, '...women hold about $900 billion of the $1.5 trillion in student loan debt."*

In the 2020 Consumer Literacy Survey, it states, [1]*"Only 16% of all U.S. adults say they have never had any debt, and of the 84% of U.S. adults who have ever had debt: Nearly 7 in 10 (69%) find it difficult to minimize their debt, primarily due to unexpected financial emergencies (23%)."* Having any category of debt brings on many emotions, struggles, and all this influences the decisions that are made to try to pay them.

Queen, for all it's worth, I know we tend to criticize those in the highest level of government when they tackle debt problems with temporary solutions because we know that in the long run, they will turn into gigantic conflicts. And rightfully so! Politicians often do not care about problems beyond the set term of their directed agendas. Therefore, they prefer to address more pressing agenda items with what they deem as immediate solutions, even if they are much worse for the country's financial future.

Look at the current news surrounding student loan forgiveness to help ease the financial burden for millions. But what is the long-term impact of doing so? What about those of us who have paid our student loans or don't even qualify for forgiveness? Is this the right solution or is the entire system flawed?

I would say the latter and it makes sense to figure out a way that is not putting millions of people in debt. I don't have all the answers, but forgiving trillions of student loan debt is not the answer, because someone has to pay for it one way or another at some point in time. You don't have to do the same with your life. You have to find a solution to your financial problem. It cannot be temporary, but final.

A Queen's Nugget of Wisdom -

> *"You either do what is hard and succeed or do what is easy and live in mediocrity." - Eric Thomas*

Evaluate and Take Responsibility

Taking responsibility for our mess is never an easy thing to do. After all, no one wants to feel like a failure. During my season of unemployment, I felt defeated. I had given eight years of solid contribution to a company only to have them say thank you, but today is your last day; without any warning. In hindsight, I had only myself to blame. I put my financial future in the hands of an employer and the government (unemployment).

I'll be the first to raise my hand and admit I got sucked into societal norms. I got sucked into the hype of building credit and having things that I really couldn't afford. I also acknowledge that practical money conversations were not held in my household growing up. No one sat me down and showed me how to budget, save, or tell me not to accumulate debt.

As I matured, I asked questions in other areas of my life, but I did not ask wise financial questions. There is an old saying that if you don't ask, you won't know. It is important when assessing what went wrong to be as honest as you can about why you are currently in financial debt.... and it's not completely someone else's fault. The more I acknowledge what steps I could have taken that I did not take, gives more power and choice in changing the outcome of my financial picture.

Queen, your debt may be a result of other factors.

Some of the factors I discovered when being honest with myself included: spending at an uncontrolled rate by not putting off immediate satisfaction, taking on higher commitments than can be faced, miscalculating the numbers in my bank account, trying to live up to peer pressures, making myself believe my job was loyal and I would never be without one, just to name a few.

It is difficult to admit: "I am the one who made the wrong decisions," but doing so is a great first step in freeing yourself from mental bondage.

It is also very difficult to admit the situation caught me off guard, because for 15 years, I depended on my salary and thought the more I earned, the more I spent. I never kept a consistent budget for my expenses. I never left my comfort zone. I did not dedicate myself to other financial possibilities, like a business; and I wasted money on things that were more liabilities than assets.

This unfortunately is common for many, so you are not alone. Once I had taken a critical look at my situation and admitted my mistakes and failures,

I had to step forward. I had to get to a point where I needed to release myself from the wrong decisions I made, forgive myself, and move forward. By affirming that I was not my past money mistakes and pursuing greater for my life. I had to do the work and realize it was not too late for me to make better choices.

That could have never happened if I didn't stop dwelling on my negative thoughts. I'm not saying it was easy. There were many, many, nights of drowning in my sorrow. My spiritual understanding of who I was and whose I was, gave me hope. I needed to affirm that financial health and wealth were possible. On many occasions, I found solace in biblical scriptures to give me hope. Psalm 23, "*the Lord is my shepherd I lack nothing*," and to affirm my vision was Jeremiah 23, "*for I know the plans I have for you saith the Lord, plans to prosper you and give you a hope and a future*." Just saying these verses and keeping my mind focused on this thought helped to move me to the next level; to make more Queen Moves.

Affirm: I am capable of overcoming any money obstacles that stand in my way. - Yvonne Brown

Queen nugget of wisdom: Devise an Action Plan (Oh Yes YOU CAN!)

Whether you had full or partial responsibility for the accumulation of your debt, you should still work to devise a plan to get out of the toxic relationship. YES, the toxic relationship. The reality of debt can be very, very depreciating, and one of the things that can cost you the most stress. Make a conscious decision to change the behavior. That requires you to eliminate all the unhealthy, messy, toxic elements that are not necessary.

Consider this, those who change their behavior for the better are the ones that quickly understand when they can say yes and when they can say no to people or things. Devise a written plan, and implement it ASAP. You have to do the same with your finances, decide to take action, cut costs, generate more income, set boundaries. Have a BY ANY LEGAL MEANS NECESSARY state of mind, I call it accountability; so that the fulfillment of your plan comes to fruition.

A budget should be part of this plan. It's the blueprint to success. I know some gurus who frown on a budget because they feel it restricts your money. I say it doesn't restrict your money; it gives your money a job. That's right your money needs to work for you, not against you. So give it an assignment and let it work. Someone who is trying to change bad behavior needs a budget to help form good habits; a budget is a way to do so.

The backbone of a successful money management plan is a budget, it's a blueprint to your financial success. If you don't remember anything at all from this chapter, remember this, making progress towards better money management includes a plan for how to allocate money.

Affirm*: I will conquer my money goals*

Queen nugget of wisdom: Challenge Your Self-Limiting Beliefs About Money

I'm sure you can tell by now, I'm all about affirmations.

Yes, affirmations played a huge part in my healing, self-love, my deliverance from financial woes and helped to remove my self-limiting beliefs. It can do the same for you, Queen, by doing the following:

If you are feeling stuck in your financial situation and can't bring yourself to start a budget, you need to dig deep...yes deep.. so let's look a little internally to challenge your beliefs about money.

Self-limiting beliefs can impact every aspect of how we think about debt, saving cash, and the purchases we make. The key is to recognize how these beliefs influence your day-to-day decisions surrounding money. Then change the behaviors they create.

Stop Saying:

1. *If I Made More Money then I Wouldn't Have any Debt, or if I Made More Money, then I Could Pay My Debt Off*
2. *A Loan is the Only Way to Purchase a Vehicle*
3. *I'm just not very good with allocating my money*

Instead, I want you to say the ***Affirm & Pursue Creed***:

> ***Affirm:*** *I am not my past money mistakes, I am my present money resolve and will move forward wisely handling my finances to create a positive relationship with money.*
>
> ***Pursue:*** *I will seek after wise counsel when I need help in the areas of money matters and will no longer dwell in uncertainty. It's my peace that offers understanding.*
>
> ***Express Gratitude:*** *I am grateful for the steps I have taken today to come into alignment with my past, present, and future and will now work towards the plan to assign value to my dollars.*

Societal norms may have programmed your mind about how money should be handled, but you can begin anew. Debt Freedom is doable! Changing your financial narrative is possible. Your strategy has to be so insane it'll leave you in disbelief but happier when you see the progress you are making. Delay unnecessary expenses as much as possible and increase your debt payments. This will require intense focus but can be accomplished.

When I decided to move impediments out of my way and change my financial narrative, I had to remove any emotional attachment to money and see it for what it is, a resource that can help me multiply my way to financial freedom. So, Queen, your plan has to be intentional, it has to reflect a S.M.A.R.T (Specific, Measurable, Achievable, Relevant, Timely) goal that will get you to your desired outcome. It must align with your belief system and how you view money. The beautiful thing about money mistakes is the opportunity to pivot and try again. Are you ready to begin anew? Do this exercise, turn to a new slate and say with conviction,

"***I AM READY TO BEGIN ANEW***."

Queen, you are in charge of your future and so the rewrite begins with you. Take some time and work through these steps.

It's time to create a new narrative. Let's Begin.

1. Identify your **money story**.

2. Understand where your **story** comes from.

3. Disprove your **story.**

4. Disassociate your **self-worth** with your **net worth**.

5. Choose a new **story** and act on it.

6. Commit to small **changes**.

7. Be willing to forgive yourself.

8. Visualize your habits. Habits will set you up for much success

Queen, I applaud you. Celebrate this step. When you begin to *crush debt* as I like to say, whether you have small, medium, large, single, or multiple debts, remember only you, with your strength and determination, can achieve your debt payoff goal.

Affirm: *Today I commit to living my financial dreams*

Get To The Root Cause Of The Problem

We start by spending more than what we earn, and then, without really realizing what is going on, the day comes when suddenly we feel crushed under the weight of debts. It's precisely at this stage that the question starts, "*How can I get out of deb*t?" Stress inevitably increases, and, in some cases, you end up losing sleep. The feeling is that of when you lack air to breathe. It becomes difficult to talk about it with others, especially with your family. In the meantime, shame rises. Ladies, I know about the shame!

We try to continue a normal life as if nothing happened. Inside, however, there is only one fix and pounding thought. Yet, if it has reached the level where debt is no longer sustainable, something will have happened. But what? Among the main causes of being overloaded with debt, we find out that we:

- Spend more than what we earn
- Try to reach a standard of living that is too high for our pockets aka LIFESTYLE INFLATION

- Pay off debts with other debts
- Use debt for recurring expenses
- Don't do any financial planning
- Suddenly lose our jobs

Fortunately, there is a remedy, and indeed there are a few. Let's see what they are.

The Action Plan - Part II

Having a plan to build a solid financial kingdom is what allows you to maintain good financial health. I'm all about the plan, so let's continue to build from the one mentioned previously. Thinking about cutting your debts a little at a time or simply based on luck will not get you anywhere. Sorry, trying to win the scratch card or lottery is a waste of time and more money. You have to roll up your sleeves and face the main problem.

To get out of the vicious cycle of debt, you must, therefore, change your attitude. If you have always behaved in the same way and this has given you these results, the time has come to try to reshuffle the cards and take a different direction.

Your number one public enemy is the principal. If you take that down, you get rid of the chains aka the interest. If, on the other hand, you only pay interest, you will continue to pay the debt indefinitely. Your only goal, should you have it, is to clear the debt as soon as possible. I will present several *Queen Moves* in this book. Whichever technique you decide to use, you must keep in mind this nugget of wisdom - you must cut down the principal portion of the debt and recover your peace as quickly as possible.

Do check us out at ***GROUP.AFFIRMANDPURSUE.COM*** for additional financial tips and resources, but the steps below will get you started.

Basic Techniques to Get Out of Debt

Rationalize Expenses: You must revisit your spending habits to recover the useful portions to deal with some of the techniques described below. It is not an easy thing; I understand, but it is necessary.

Pay yourself first. As soon as you receive income, you must allocate a certain percentage for your future long term needs and expenses, and then allocate what you want to use to pay for necessities, short-term savings and to pay off the debts.

In this way, you will be able to revisit any additional expenses to ensure ends meet because your goal is to save money without having to cut everything and without a sense of guilt.

Queen Nugget of Wisdom: Give Your Money A Job. Let Your Money Work for You. Not Against You. - ASSIGN EVERY DOLLAR, DOWN TO THE PENNY

No More Debt: If you want to reduce and cancel your debts, you must avoid opening new ones to pay the old ones. Continuing to do this is like a dog biting its tail; it will never come to an end. This step may seem simple, but it is not, especially when you see how easy it is to get it. I got my first credit card in college and to this day I don't know how that was possible, but I did and it set off a chain of more credit cards and more offers because my creditor saw how responsible I was with managing debt and as a result, I had a good credit score as a result of managing the debt. I won't go deep into credit in this book, but just know that access to lines of credit was based on *my ability to manage debt well.*

This habit is very dangerous because the more you accumulate debts and of course pay them off, the more you will be solicited for new financing opportunities, exposing you to any disclosure of the assets given as collateral. You will also reach a limit beyond which no bank or financial company will be willing to extend credit to you. The good ole debt-to-income ratio. Ladies, trust me when I say it will happen, it can happen because it has to me!

Remember: Financial education is a lifetime commitment. Money Management is 80% behavior and 20% logic.

Anyone who comes to me for help, I share the one tried and true method that has helped me pay off debt without hesitation. You may have heard of it:

The "Snowball": The "Snowball" technique is extremely effective and increases your satisfaction level exponentially. The concept is simple. If you take a little snow and gather it in your hands forming a small ball and then you "roll" it down the mountain, gradually the ball will increase in volume and, once it reaches the valley, it will have become huge.

Here, you have to recreate the same effect. Make a list of all your debts from the smallest to the largest in terms of principal to be repaid as in the examples below. If two debts have similar debt amounts, select the one with the highest interest rate first. After that, concentrate all the resources you have available to repay the principal portion of the smallest debt while for the others, you pay the bare minimum (maybe even just the interest portion). Whenever you close a debt, use additional resources to attack the principal portion of the next debt, and so on. You will see that each step will increase your saving capacity and, therefore, action. If you want, you can use the ready-made and set file that I prepared for this technique.

Cut Credit Cards: I know this strategy is not popular and uncomfortable because our system is built on credit. Please know this is how this country is built on capitalism. It's built on the 700 and the 800 scores to get the house, the car, the loan. I know cutting the card is not what you want to do, HOWEVER, if we can be honest, these plastic cards are one of the main causes of excessive debt. Anyway, they are used for the wrong reason, like shopping for the purchase of non necessities. Especially revolving lines of credit cards, which are very dangerous because you end up paying very high and ever-increasing rates.

If you know you can't be responsible for managing credit, you must cut them immediately and cancel them. Credit cards are not an additional income stream. If canceling them scares you, then at least cut them up so you are not tempted to use them until you have paid down the debt and changed your behavior.

And here's another Queen nugget I want to add here. If you pay interest, your hard-earned coins are funding someone else's credit card. That is how the lenders are making money, in a risk-free way. If you don't get a clear understanding of how this concept works and can cripple you, you will forever pay for it with your money in the form of interest. Yes, Queen, the lender (the bank) uses your interest to fund other things, not you. For this reason, you need not put yourself in a situation where you keep owing someone else.

Paying in Cash: For a while, you have to force yourself to always pay everything in cash. No more ATMs, no more online payments, and, of course, no more credit cards. Only cash. In this way, you will have a greater awareness of what you are spending and, above all, greater control.

Having to physically make all the cash payments, you will have to constantly withdraw and see the money come out of the wallet, which will give you more strength in taking control of the situation. Avoid making payments online (for example, Amazon), but going physically in the stores will avoid many purchases. Guaranteed.

Listen, I realize this step may require some flexibility due to the current state of things in our economy, so I will say if you are not comfortable shopping in a physical store and want to purchase things online, have a designated debit card for that specific amount and that's it. But it needs to be a debit NOT a credit card. Once you have spent the allocated amount - remember to give your dollars an assignment - that's it.

CAUTION! If you are not strong enough to handle this step, then ask someone you trust to help you. I know the thought of using a card, even though it is a debit card may not be easy as a first step when you are trying to change the behavior, but I say to get help from someone who can help you shop, as I know there may be some hesitation with going into a physical store at this time.

Apply Additional Amounts: Again, your #1 goal is to cut the principal portion of your debts. For this reason, all additional monies you receive must go in that direction, none excluded (ex: work bonuses, prizes, inheritance, gift, tax bonus, etc.). All the excess (as I like to call it) recovered must be added as part of your only goal: to reduce the debt.

Selling Unused Items: With this technique, you achieve two goals. On the one hand, you recover useful resources to settle your debts and, on the other hand, empty the garage, your closet, or the cellar, which is not all this bad.

No matter what amount you collect, deposit it into an account separate from the one you normally use for your expenses, and when you have reached a good level, you already know what to do. This strategy has been useful to me and was instrumental in paying off my student debt in 2020. #winning

Other Things To Consider:

Stimulus Money - Put at least some of it in your emergency fund

Tax Refund - if you are getting a refund, save it

That's a good start and then take a look at your budget for expenses you can cut:

Anything you don't need to get by

Anything you forgot you were paying for

Anything you can get for free

Anything you can't use right now

An emergency fund will ensure you do not fall back into the temptation to use debt for unforeseen expenses. It is your go-to fund when an unplanned expense occurs. Go to this fund first to take care of the emergency and then replenish it as soon as you can.

[1]The Harris Poll, 2020 Financial Literacy Survey, March 23, 2020

For additional complimentary bonuses: Download your monthly budget workbook at bonus.affirmandpursue.com. Use Coupon Code: FREE

EXERCISE: How Much Money Are You Giving Away?

Monthly Income After Taxes	

Monthly Payment Amounts	
Mortgage	
Primary Home	
Home Equity	
2nd/Reverse Mortgage	
Additional Properties	

Car Note	
Student Loans	
Personal Loans	
Line of Credit	

Credit Cards	
Name	**Monthly Amount**
Misc (Furniture, Equipment, Jewelry	

Total Monthly Debt Payments	

(Total Monthly Debt Payments / Monthly Income After Taxes) X 100 = Debt To Income Ratio

I, ___________________ willingly and freely give away $______________ dollars every month, which is ____ percent of my hard earned income. I need to be delivered from debt.

Crush debt by any legal means necessary - Yvonne Brown

Chapter 2: Budgeting: How to Effectively Spend Your Money

A monthly budget is a blueprint to help guide you and allocate your money -Yvonne Brown

One of the things I have learned is that you must be willing to make a short-term sacrifice for greater financial gain. The thing you sacrifice now won't seem taxing over time, because you are building steps and habits and with anything habitual, you will get better with it. This includes the importance of a budget, to help guard your mind AND control spending.

A monthly budget is a tool that helps you determine and control the expenses you make more frequently month by month. When you have clear data, you can manage your money more optimally. If you want to know how to make a simple and effective monthly budget, you must know that expenses are divided into:

Fixed Expenses: Those that are made every month and that does not have a significant variation in terms of amounts. This category includes the costs of services, rent, loans, tuition, etc. When I consider these types of expenses, it is my mortgage, insurance, etc.

Variable Expenses: They are those that vary monthly as well as their values. Here, you can find expenses incurred due to festivities, outings to restaurants, clothing, entertainment, and fuel, among others. When I consider these types of expenses it is eating out, going to buy shoes or clothing, manicures, pedicures, etc. When making budget adjustments, you must pay attention to this section. This section of my budget was the area where I could cut things that were not NEEDs but more WANTs.

Subtract expenses from income to equal zero: The idea is that you can achieve a balance between income and expenses that allows you to have positive balances (surplus). Remember it is important to budget every dollar or assign it to a line item. If you find that the flow of liquidity (cash) is negative, you have to make the respective changes to your lifestyle, reducing those expenses that are less important.

If, on the other hand, cash is positive, you can use these resources to increase capital through savings, paying off debt, or investments. Regarding the above, it is recommended that you consider a percentage to allocate to savings that work for you, as all incomes and expenses are not created equal; but please ensure the necessities that you need to survive are taken into account first.

Creating a monthly budget that allows you to monitor expenses, it isn't always easy, but with practice and consistency, it will become routine. If you focus on increasing your income, depending on the excess amount you have, you can make adjustments such as increasing the dollar value you allocate to savings to have more capital. Currently, there are different tools to prepare more advanced budgets according to your needs. Excel and Google Sheets templates are useful tools and if you are the type of person that enjoys spreadsheets and formulas, then go for it. There are also various apps that you can use. I have used various ways to create a budget, pen to paper, spreadsheet (I have an amazing budgeting worksheet as part of my financial workbook bonuses); I also use the Every Dollar app. All three methods have worked for me, you'll need to find what works for you and get started.

For additional complimentary bonuses: Download your monthly budget workbook at bonus.affirmandpursue.com. Use Coupon Code: FREE

When you take on a Queen mindset, incorporating these tools offers you the opportunity to prioritize what you consume and means to achieve the goals you previously established. Queen, it is not enough to simply plan a budget and prepare it. There is a saying, "failing to prepare, we prepare to fail."

So planning to do the budget is a necessary part of building the foundation of your financial kingdom.

Keep the following tips in mind:

Reassess your budget periodically (at least every 3 months)

The key element here is establishing consistency in reviewing your plan. Change is a necessary function of life. So re-assessment of the budget plan and making necessary adjustments will help you maintain progress. If you do not update your budget monthly, you risk returning to old negative habits that don't work and keep you stuck in financial prison. Monitoring the budget allows you to measure the effectiveness of the adjustments you make.

For example, I am a big proponent of keeping my expenses low. There was a warranty item in my budget that had always been a recurring line item. However, after much thought and weighing the pros and cons of this service, I decided based on where I am currently with the need for this service, it no longer added value. I am now able to take the $60.00 I allocated for the warranty and put it in my emergency fund. This makes more sense to me than paying the warranty company for something that had a slight chance of occurring during the year.

Be accurate with the information - *"Accuracy Builds Credibility"* - Jim Rohn

It is wise to include as much data as you can about your expenditures monthly. What you don't account for provides an inaccurate picture of what your needs are and what you can spend. It also affects your ability to make wise financial decisions. This can have a snowball effect. Consider finding an accountability partner that can help/encourage you to be accurate and honest about your financial state. Remember, Queens are women who can face curveballs and crises with perseverance and tenacity.

Implement a realistic spending plan

For this Queen move to work, you have to be honest with yourself and your accountability partner about how much you bring in monthly and what your monthly expenses are. If, for example, you see the need to cut your hair bi-weekly, but do not include any figures in your budget to represent this, it is evident there will be a mismatch between what you spend and the budget estimate you made.

Maintain discipline

Any activity you do requires discipline to be successful. As for your finances, this value is important since you must commit to sticking to the budget to the letter. Now, if for some reason you do not meet your monthly goals, do not get discouraged, you always have the opportunity to continue with the work and get better the more you do it. Remember, mistakes make masters.

Protect savings

As the popular saying goes: "She who keeps always has." Never ignore the importance of saving as one of the objectives that you should look for when making the budget. If you have an excess amount, increase what you allocate to savings, since increasing this figure will only bring you financial benefits.

Financial stability is a dream that many people seek to achieve. However, it is not an impossible dream with the wealth of tangible and intangible resources available so that you can build your wealth, manage your money well, keep your finances healthy, and organize your activities based on a budget with high degrees of effectiveness.

Hence, if you maintain the right attitude and desire, you can overcome any financial difficulty that comes your way. Knowing how to make and manage a monthly budget is an important element of personal finance.

Money Management

Since its inception, money has generated controversy about its real value and there are still grumblings about the US dollar holding its value. But that's another topic for another day. Many individuals have a "toxic relationship" with money. A lot of ills have come as a result of how money is handled. The truth is that money is only a means; in other words, money is what brings us benefits and can help avoid problems when handled correctly. Money is important because it determines where we live, what we drive, clothes we wear, how and where we can travel, and when we can retire. Therefore, it is a resource that should be handled wisely.

Money Management is About Forming Habits

Queen, I thought I was handling my money wisely until unemployment came knocking on my door and I quickly saw that my behavior, my relationship with money was not healthy. What about you? What is your behavior as it relates to money management?

If you think about how to manage your money, you consider that a fundamental factor is the size of your salary or income. Of course, it influences your money decisions, but it is not entirely decisive. Money management can be done from any budget regardless of income. If you don't believe it, consider this: a company with a large initial budget can look just as bankrupt as a citizen who started with a small budget. Why?

Because money management is 80% behavior and 20% logic.

Therefore, the one thing that you constantly ask yourself about the correct way to manage your money is to be intentional with the choices made and pay attention to how it is allocated since it will help you to cover unforeseen expenses, achieve economic independence; know exactly how much you have, avoid debts, and get to manifesting your dreams - getting you to your desired state; financial freedom.

Managing money is key to making it yield and grow. Sometimes it seems that the money was not enough for us or that, when it comes down to it, we have it earmarked for a multitude of things, and we end up spending it without knowing. It's not a surprise to have this type of mindset. If you can be honest with yourself, money management is not taught in secondary schools nor colleges, or universities. Guess what?? I have two business degrees and didn't take not one course that taught me about personal finance, how to manage my money, and manage it to make it grow. I have nephews in high school as of this writing and ask them what classes they are taking and it is not anything about money. It is up to us who know better, to do better and inform the next generation of the importance of proper money management so they don't fall prey to the same mistakes. Plant the seeds NOW!

Queen, getting into the habit of managing it every month. It is an excellent opportunity to increase your wealth. Many people do not believe that it is so important to look at the details, but I can't stress enough that you need to be joined at the hip as it relates to your hard-earned coins (as I like to call them). Don't let anyone deter you or tell you it is wrong, be religious about your money, write down your money goals, your projects, your income minus your expenses to get a clear picture of how good or bad you are with your finances. The reality is that the people who are most aware of their money are the ones who can effectively manage it in a way that makes it grow. And we are going to see step by step how we can achieve it in our lives:

Keep Track of All Your Money

Your normal, unexpected income, and extra income, etc. Even if they are very few, no matter how you obtained them, all the money that enters your life, you should write it down. Why is this important? Because many times we do not realize where the money is going, what we spend it on, or how much money it means to have certain habits such as having a daily coffee or tea. Listen, Starbucks is my favorite place to grab a vanilla chai tea with almond milk, BUUUUTTTTTT I had to check myself and sacrifice the daily consumption when I saw where my money was going.

Some people spend even thousands of dollars a year on just coffee. Don't let this be you. If you must have your daily dose of coffee, maybe you buy wholesale or when or sale (use that coupon). Still not convinced how much your spending, transactions will tell it all. So check your bank account LOL! You will realize how you are handling money and identify opportunities that would otherwise have gone unnoticed by you.

2. Budget For Everything

Let's suppose that you want to carry out certain fun or entertaining activities every month. For example, go to the cinema, travel to another place, etc. Well, all that should be budgeted. Many times when perhaps we have a job or are earning money, we simply make money for something because we feel we deserve it. And we deserve it. However, the idea is that all of this is planned and budgeted because when it is not, we usually tend to spend a little more than normal.

So the idea is that you do the following: If you are going on vacation, think: "I can get more or less 200 dollars in it"(or whatever amount). And then you carry more or less that amount you're budgeting for. If for some reason, you went over budget, then you'll wonder what happened, what was it that you overspent, etc. Later, when you are planning another outing, you will already have better data to conclude the forecasted costs based on what was spent prior. That ability to predict how much you are going to spend money on certain things, be it fun, work, spending with your children, or anything else, is essential because it allows you to be in control and to be able to decide consciously if it is something suitable or not for you at that moment from a financial point of view.

3. Pay Debts

It is obvious. Paying debts is part of good financial management. Here are a few things to keep in mind:

Acquire No More Financial Obligations

If you are heavily in debt at this time, do everything you can to avoid acquiring more debt. This is essential. Many people, even though they know they are in debt, know how bad it is to have debts, perhaps in default and not having been able to pay or are aware of the amount of interest so high that they pay month by month. Despite this, they suddenly think that they want to treat themselves or take a vacation, and they get into more debt. Or maybe they want to upgrade to the latest computer or iPhone instead of being satisfied with what they have unless it is truly on its last leg and they have no choice but to buy new equipment. Even if that was the case, do not acquire any more debt. Buy what you can afford and it doesn't have to be the latest and greatest gadget on the market and still be able to meet your needs.

Remember money management is 80% behavior and 20% logic.

Acquire the Habit of Paying Capital Every Month

What do I mean by "pay capital"? In case you do not know the term, it refers to the following: Usually, when you have a debt with a bank or some entity, you pay a monthly fee that is usually called the "minimum fee," which usually includes a portion that goes to interest (which is what the bank receives for having loaned you money). And another portion that is accumulating for the total balance of your debt until you finish (this is the capital).

As it turns out if you add a little more, for example, 10% or 20% more than what you are paying, you are bringing forward the payment of future installments, but without interest. For example, let's say you have a debt for which you must pay $500 per month and there are $200 interest and $300 of capital. Now, for the capital portion, you do not pay $500 every month, but $600.

It turns out, in five months, you pay the equivalent of one installment (from $100 that you are adding additional), but all those $500 go to principal and nothing to interest. In other words, in three months, you would have paid one full installment of capital, just increasing a little more than what you pay per month. In your particular case, it doesn't matter if you can only increase $10, $5, or $20 each month. The important thing is to get into the habit of doing it every month with as much money as possible.

Always have the goal in mind to be 100% debt-free

There is a scripture that says, "Owe no man nothing". This applies and should be followed. Becoming debt-free is not for the faint of heart but with a plan and focus, it is doable. The sweet spot is once you have achieved it, now you can use the money towards something meaningful like building your savings or investing. Because you own no one anything.

Maybe you who have read this far and are not in debt, which is great. However, there is also a powerful idea for you, and that is that you make an account as if you were in debt, and every month you pay something of what you earn so you earn a little. Simply when you receive some money, allocate a portion to savings. This is a habit that will allow you to accomplish many things later. Financial habits are what allow people to achieve financial success and abundance.

4. Plan Your Expenses In Advance

Usually, we have the same expenses monthly, almost always with the same budget: buying food, paying for certain services, renting, children's school, etc. However, the idea is as follows: before the month starts and before you start keeping track of your finances (if you haven't already), you have to account for how much you think you'll spend monthly, that even includes budgeting for unforeseen events or fun things you like to do.

For example, suppose this would be your expenses:

- Mortgage/Rent: 1200
- Energy bill: $200
- Water bill: $240
- Transportation fee: $200
- Gasoline for the car: $200
- Food: $300
- Selfcare: $260
- Debt: $500 dollars

- Entertainment: $100

Total: $3200

Once you have this number, then take into account all the income you will receive and subtract the expenses from this number. At the end of the month, you should review your budgeted expenses against what you spent. You may shout for joy or be disappointed, but the goal here is awareness of how you are handling your money. This exercise will help you to adjust any unnecessary expenses OR look to bring in additional income so you are not going over your budgeted amount. This reconciliation has been very instrumental in keeping me honest with my finances. It will become second nature the more you do it.

Accounting for everyday expenses or income sounds exhausting, but once you find your rhythm, it will become easier like a well-oiled machine. Ladies, flowing this way will be like clockwork once you get going and can know more or less monthly where your money is going. That is the power of a budget! It sets up a boundary for you and others. Why? You have a picture of what you can and cannot spend or give to others.

True Financial Freedom Mentality

This tip is not so much for managing money, but it is a type of mentality that I would like you to acquire regarding it. Many people talk about the importance of budgeting and saving and how essential it is every month. And that's fine, I recommend it.

Queen, there is no limit to the amount of money you can save, especially with the right strategy AND there is never a limit to the amount of money you can earn. For example, many people complain about the minimum wage, but it turns out that while people are earning the minimum wage, there are people who are earning 10 times the minimum wage, 20 times, and even 100 times doing other kinds of things.

It may be necessary to change your job for a higher salary, acquire new skills, and do different things to increase your income and hence your savings.

Take the limits off and begin to define what true financial freedom means for you. Only you can determine what that is and if it looks like it includes additional income streams, then it's time to take action.

To learn more about increasing your income by having additional income streams check out my book: ***Money Matters For Side Hustles: A 12 Step Guide Starting A Side Hustle*** available at www.yvonnebrownexhales.com.

Increase your income; keep your expenses low., KEY!! Live on less than you make - Yvonne Brown

5. Keep Your Emotions In Check

That is, you must have absolute control over what you are spending your money on. Some things are unnecessary; others are perhaps mere desires. AKA Needs vs Wants. Perhaps the temptation to buy junk food, that pair of shoes/sneakers, more clothes,etc. Emotional spending can get you in trouble. When you control your emotions, you not only acquire the ability to save a little more money, not to spend so much on vain things, but you also acquire self-control, and this is fundamental because, in money, many excellent decisions come from self-control.

Dealing With Debts

Debts are the norm in the capitalistic country. But it doesn't have to be your norm. Ok, yes I know what we are told about debt, but let's change the narrative and negate anything that hinders our financial freedom. When debts exceed your ability to pay, they become negative and can cause you great headaches. There is a health cost to being in debt. Unfortunately, this country is built on debt, and owes so much to others but that doesn't need to be you and shouldn't be you. Remember what I mentioned above, "Owe No Man Nothing." One of the main causes of debt, is people spend much more money than they receive. The difference between expenditure and income causes one to be in debt, but this type of debt undoubtedly has to do with a lack of knowledge about finances.

Lack of knowledge about payments: Debts are a responsibility that should not be taken lightly. That is why if you are going to acquire any debt, you must be sure that you can make the payments. Above all, make sure that payment is made on time. When we do not make payments on time, our credit history is affected.

Lack of knowledge about the minimum payment: When paying any debt, they always offer you the minimum payment option with which many people believe that they can easily get out of some type of debt. Paying the minimum of our debts only makes them longer, and the interest can increase. You should always pay more than the minimum payment and, if possible, settle the account in the shortest time.

Lack of knowledge about purchases: Buying without having real knowledge about the things that we are going to acquire causes indebtedness. Not knowing about the offers that we can find or making a comparison will make us overspend.

Lack of financial tools: Not being interested or informed about the good management of finances can also lead to debt. Financial tools help you create a healthy economic future. Try to find out about them.

Other Causes of Debt

In addition to lack of knowledge, other causes can put your finances at risk or cause you to get into debt.

Too many cards: Using a credit card can be risky when we are not disciplined. There are trillions of people in credit card debt because the way the money system is set up is to keep us broke. Keep us wanting lavish things, keep us overextending ourselves for things we really can't afford or cash would've been the first tender used for purchases.

Lack of financial management: In our daily life, the acquisition of goods and services is common, but if we acquire these without prior planning or a budget, then we run the risk of not having control and getting into debt.

Impulse purchases: A common activity in today's world, buying just because it was a great deal or because it was the last chance, the only date, etc. Falling into advertising networks is very easy, especially when we are not clear on the difference between our wishes and our real needs. Because something is on sale or is a liquidation season, it does not force you to purchase any product. Buy products you need and when the purchases are very large, then take advantage of the discounts.

Rhino's Secret: Attack and Eliminate Your Debt

The Rhino's weapon is to attack. When he feels threatened, he searches for the greatest threat and attacks it by taking control of the situation quickly. Rhinos are fairly peaceful and do not have many enemies, although the mother rhino must often defend her young from multiple predators and dangers. Therefore, she must also evaluate her options. The only option you don't have is not to deal with the dangers.

What does the rhino generally do when presented with a danger? Attack the predator to protect yourself. It is the same with your money. You have to manage the level of debt you take on to make sure it doesn't threaten your financial security.

Because debt is so expensive, and you eat so much of your wealth, you must find ways to reduce it quickly and always manage it carefully. Debt only becomes unmanageable if it consumes a large part of your monthly income and it's paid down too slowly.

Identify the risks, difficulties, limitations, and unforeseen events that affect a budget and explain the consequences of poor financial planning. Understand how to attack your debt and the consequences of not doing so. Getting out of debt can be one of the most difficult challenges in life, but it is also one of the most important achievements you can have.

To wrap up this chapter, let me assure you that I am determined to pay off my debt. While it hasn't been easy, the wins experienced, as I pay off one balance and then another, is so refreshing and has given me much to exhale about. I always say it is important to crush debt. YES CRUSH IT!

Three Reasons Why I Will Continue To Crush Debt:

- ✓ It Robs Me Of My Peace
- ✓ It Increases My Net Worth
- ✓ Interest Is Not Paid To Me

There are many more reasons but these are the top three that I keep in the forefront of my thoughts daily. Queen, what are your main reasons? If you haven't come up with any, take time now before moving on to the next chapter to ask yourself why you are determined to pay off debt. No rush, take your time, and write it down below. When you're done, proceed to chapter 3.

Three Reasons Why I Will Crush Debt:

1.

2.

3.

Chapter 3: Saving Habits and Investing

Being disciplined and consistent with your decisions is paramount to financial success; there is no magic formula.
- Yvonne Brown

A Queen's Nugget of Wisdom--Queen Moves - we save, save, save

Look around you and see that the world you once knew is no longer in existence. The job you started last year, last month, maybe today is different. There is a saying that change is constant; however, some changes have a significant impact and some have minimal impact. The Covid-19 Pandemic has had a significant, worldwide impact. As a result of this unexpected change, many corporations and businesses are simply trying to stay afloat. Changes such as the Covid-19 Pandemic, death, loss of health, taking on caring for additional family members, and many other unanticipated changes are good reasons to adopt the habit of saving money. Changes you can deal with are easier to deal with; it is often the unanticipated changes that are often the most difficult changes to adjust to. Unanticipated changes are a part of life; they happen whether we want them to or not.

Queen, in March 2020, the company I worked for was impacted by the effects of the pandemic and this directly affected me; but not as much as the loss of a job I had experienced earlier in my life. Because of that experience, I was more prepared for this unanticipated change; but it still had its impact. As a result of the Pandemic, the company laid off most of its employees; those who were not laid off suffered a 70% cut in salary with additional work being requested of them. I was not laid off; yes, you read it correctly, 70% off my gross income was gone and I still had to do multiple jobs. I'll go on record and say, **YOUR JOB AIN'T LOYAL!**

What kind of deal was I given?! It isn't one and that is why the content in Queen Moves is so important. Should you be impacted by downsizing or termination, how much savings do you have? Let me say this, unemployment income is not enough. I am a living witness. You need a cushion to help buffer the loss in your finances because once again, **a job is not loyal**. I learned that hard lesson in 2013 and once I got back on my feet, I began to take this habit more seriously for this very reason.

I started from zero but now have enough to cover my expenses for 6 months. I made some sacrificial changes to save. I decided to move back home which helped me save on the normal utility expenses and I also decided to rent my home, so any funds I receive goes towards debt and savings. It's a WIN-WIN for me! So when my salary was cut by 70%, because I had been living on less for some time to redirect what I would've paid in cable, subscriptions, gym membership, recurring monthly expenses, I no longer concerned myself with those costs and instead chose to redirect to either debt or savings. You see when you save for a rainy day, you are putting yourself in a better financial situation so you are not tempted to use a credit card or take out a loan when the unexpected happens.

Up to this point, I have discussed the importance of forming healthy habits such as: changing your mindset, budgeting, assessing your debt, and crushing it. Adopting these tools and using them consistently creates the space to consider an additional habit that will move you closer to building financial stability and wealth: the habit of saving money. Nobody changes a habit overnight, right? Neuroscientists report that it takes at least 21 days for our brain to get used to our routines. Therefore, consistently saving money is the most important behavioral change to adopt when it comes to creating the habit of saving money. It is more important to consistently save than how much you save monthly. Once you have successfully adopted this habit, you can then reassess an increase in the amount you are saving monthly. Be CONSISTENT!

Remember money management is 80% behavior and 20% logic.

So you know that saving and budgeting are important, but you don't know where to start? Then pay close attention to this chapter. First of all, I want to make sure you understand very well the impact that long-term savings can have: If you manage to save $1 a day in 20 years, you will accumulate more than $12,000 if you have an annual interest of 5%. Hard to believe, but it is so.

You may be wondering...well where do I begin? Begin with setting a small goal daily. To ensure success with this, the goal should be small and tangible. Some examples of small tangible goals include: Writing down what you want to save for the month or committing to not eating out for 30 days to save money. You could even set a goal to learn how to cook inexpensive but delicious meals once per week. These goals need to be tailored to your needs and your financial picture. You will need to figure out what small and tangible goals will work for you. It is the sum of mini habits that will make the difference. This is not a 100-meter run, but a 42-kilometer marathon. You don't need to accelerate. Just don't stop.

Knowing how to save money is the foundation of personal finance, and is one of the elements to achieving financial freedom. Many see it as something impossible to master as if an external element forced them to spend all their income; not so, and you are going to learn a way to save money that works.

As much as my steps can teach you, if you don't do your part, you won't save a penny. If you want to save the "typical" 10 - 15% of your salary, this way of saving money may work for you, but consistency is the key to success. Saving money every week or day by day using the right savings vehicle will make the difference. However, it just as important to:

Control Your Day-To-Day Expenses

The first step is to choose a method to control your daily expenses. I'm not asking you to start saving or thinking about ways to do it, simply that you identify what you spend your money on.

It is very tedious to quantify each of your expenses, but this is the only way to save a relevant percentage of your money.Today, it is easier than ever to have control of personal or family expenses. Once you get used to it, you don't want to stop doing it, I assure you. Doing so will allow you to know at all times where your money is going and if you are achieving the goals you have set for yourself.

Learn How to Track Your Expenses

Next, I am going to explain three ways to track your daily expenses and track household savings. Choose the one you prefer:

Financial apps: There are multiple apps, so you can surely find one that you like. I mention a few below that I recommend:

- EveryDollar -helps you create a monthly budget so you can achieve your money goals aka zero-based budgeting. [Basic: Free; Plus $] *
- Mint - providing detailed spending breakdowns and customizable budgets, you can take advantage of the "Goals" feature to help you stay on track while paying off your debt. [Free]
- Pocket Guard - Help to guard against spending too much. [Free]
- Goodbudget - Basic household money management and you can create spending "envelopes." [Basic: Free; Plus $]

Spreadsheet: Snazzy with the numbers and formulas? Then this method is for you. It's about creating a spreadsheet in Excel or Google Sheets in a way that allows you to record all your daily expenses. It's a little more complex since you must create it yourself, and it is not as handy as utilizing an app. The good thing is that you can create it to your liking. If you do not see yourself able to create your excel or google sheets, there are many free templates online.

Paper and pen: Finally, if you're not tech-savvy and prefer pen to paper, there is the possibility of recording your household expenses in the old way. It's not the most recommended since it is laborious, but if you do not see yourself able to use the other forms, this is better than nothing. What is important is the implementation!

As a matter of fact, I have one for you. Check out the bonus section for access to a free template that you can use TODAY.

How to Organize Your Expenses

Once you have chosen the way to track your expenses, you will have to define the different categories in which to organize your expenses. See an example below, but it is up to you. I recommend ensuring your NEEDS are at the top vs WANTs:

- Apartment (rent) / House (mortgage)
- Utilities (electricity, gas, water,)
- Groceries (everything we buy in the supermarket and the market)
- Transportation (Car, gasoline, insurance, and related expenses
- Internet
- Phone (cell)
- Leisure (activities, restaurants)
- Shopping (various purchases such as clothing, household items, or electronic devices)
- Travel (everything related to travel)
- Others (donations, gifts, hairdressing, blog)

Prioritize Your Savings

Once you have made a decision on which tool you are going to use to track your daily expenses, you will be able to determine how much you can realistically save and how often you can contribute to a savings fund. You will be able to prioritize your savings.

Savings can be prioritized in many ways. I am going to explain the method that has allowed me to save a great amount of money (approximately 50%). My way of doing it is by classifying the categories of expenses that we have defined into the following groups:

Main expenses: *these are the expenses that are indeed necessities, I call it the four walls of needs. In this category, there is usually the rent/mortgage, transportation, utilities, etc.*

Secondary expenses: *these are the expenses that, although they may be important, you have more margin to reduce or eliminate them. In turn, you must divide them into the following categories:*

Recurring secondary expenses: *these are expenses that recur on a weekly or monthly basis; they are a part of your habitual spending. Some examples of these include weekly supermarket purchases, restaurants (if you go often), subscriptions. They are usually monthly or annual expenses.*

Additional secondary expenses: *these are expenses that occur from time to time very infrequently. Some examples include birthday gifts, trips, and activities.*

Spending classification is a very personal thing, so these examples may not apply to you. Once you have them classified (either on paper, in excel, or a mental note), we will see the savings strategy to be followed by each group.

You may tend to classify many expenses as "main," but try to leave the essentials there. Remember that this is not a classification between fixed and variable expenses. Your number one priority will be to reduce recurring secondary expenses. First of all, you should look for any that you can directly remove. Ask yourself, "Is this a need or a want? Can I survive without this expense?" Some examples of expenses to be eliminated can be:

1. Subscription to the gym that you do not use.
2. Video/music streaming services that you do not use or could centralize in one (Spotify, Netflix, HBO, etc.).
3. Mobile insurance or others that are not necessary (although they sold them very well).
4. Monthly subscription apps that you hardly use.
5. Coffee from your favorite barista (can't you make it at home?).
6. Mani/Pedis (every two weeks, maybe DIY is the way to go for a little while)

Review each of your expenses and don't hesitate to eliminate any that are not necessary. Once you've removed and eliminated what no longer serves you, the next step is to try to reduce or optimize those that you cannot eliminate. Some examples of optimization to save are:

Reduce consumption in gas, electricity, and water in addition to canceling the additional "services" that are included in your contracts (in the case of electricity, you can lower the power as well). Here, I explain how to save on the electricity bill. Buy less internet speed (do you need 300 megabytes?) Buy more white labels and fewer processed foods (cooking is the best way to save and eat healthier). Go out to eat less if you go very often or, as an intermediate solution, order food at home (it is usually cheaper). Using public transport or the bike instead of the car (this could mean significant savings). Buy clothes only if you need them and, if possible, on sale. Hit the clearance sales!

Occasional Side Expenses (The Pop-Ups)

There will be times you cannot anticipate this type of expense, and the decision is made on the spot, so you must be prepared for when the occasion comes. To help you be fiscally responsible, you can follow some of these tips that will allow you to avoid or reduce your expenses in the future: Ask yourself: Is it really necessary to buy this or that? Could I do it myself or buy it somewhere cheaper? Let a few days pass before making any purchase to reflect on whether it is worth it (it is a very silly trick, but I assure you that it works wonderfully). Rate from 0 to 10 how happy you will do what you want to do or buy. Rate from 0 to 10 the degree of utility of what you want to do or buy.

Think about whether this expense you make is out of pure commitment and value, saying no. Analyze if it is something that involves more expenses in the future and takes the answer you come up with into account when making the decision (for example, if you buy an iPad, then every two or three years you "have" to renew it).

Finally, you have the main expenses. The main expenses are more difficult to reduce (than not impossible) without disassembling your lifestyle, and usually make up a very relevant part of your household expenses, so they cannot be neglected. I am not going to ask you to start reducing these expenses now, but you should keep in mind the expense of these items and try to think if there are alternatives. To do this, these questions will help you reflect on the main themes:

Do you need to buy a home? The flexibility of rental may perhaps allow you to save in the long term. It's a matter of crunching and then reviewing the numbers. Could you live in a smaller apartment or a cheaper area while maintaining the quality of life? Is it necessary to take the car to go to work or to make the purchase? If your job involves you living in a more expensive place, have you considered changing your job or asking to work from home and go to a cheaper place? Does a new car paid in installments make you happier than a second-hand one? Are you aware of how much they devalue once they leave the dealership? Are your children going to be happier by going to a private school? Do you need a person to clean your house?

Making Queen Moves involves making a short-term sacrifice for long-term financial gain. Making Queen Moves involves you being a little uncomfortable now so you can live in comfort later. Making Queen Moves involves intentionality and rethinking all important decisions from a financial, not emotional point of view.

REMEMBER: Success comes in CAN'S; Failures comes in CANT'S - Anonymous

Think of this Queen, sometimes a good strategy to "save" is not to increase your expenses as your salary also increases. It's to avoid so-called lifestyle inflation. On average, the salary increases 3% or more depending on experience. When this happens, what people usually do is raise their lifestyle at the same rate. The result?

People spend more and more money without being happier, making them more dependent on their jobs to support their current lifestyle. If, on the other hand, you maintain the expenses you had at a lower salary, and adopt a minimalist way of living, regardless of whether your salary increases, your savings grow, and your freedom will also increase. Additionally, when counting the positives of accepting a position that provides you additional income, be sure to count the costs... Costs can include less personal time to be creative or spend time with family and friends; keep this in mind as you advance in your professional career.

You have to be able to increase your income or decrease your expenses.

This was the mindset I had to adopt to save more and stay on track with my financial goals. I decided to move back home for a little while to do this and I am so glad I did because I was able to build my emergency fund quicker and pay off debt at a faster rate. So there is no magic to this, it's simply to increase your income or decrease your expenses. I can go more into how you can increase your income in Chapter 6.

Start Saving Money

Once you have your method of controlling household expenses and have prioritized spending, the moment of truth comes. Start saving money now. A Grow article by Shawn M. Carter states,

> [2] *"It's no surprise that the pandemic hurt Americans' finances. But even after a year of Covid, the numbers are still striking: More than half, 56%, of adults are living "paycheck to paycheck" and 43% say they are "extremely" or "very" reliant on the third round of government stimulus checks arriving this month... Whatever your financial status is, La Spisa says the chief priority should be getting your budget in order. It's all the fundamentals, he explains: Pay yourself first. Have a plan for extra cash... Try to tighten the belt and figure out what to do with your existing budget. Don't neglect immediate expenses to put extra cash toward retirement or a big purchase."*

There is not much to explain about this step. It is about eliminating or reducing the expenses you have identified. Here, the control that you have over your expenses plays a fundamental role since it will allow you to know if you are progressing towards your savings goal. Remember earlier I stated the emergency fund is paramount to begin this financial journey. At a minimum, you should have $1000 saved in an account that is easily accessible and continue to add to it as you can build 3-6 months of expenses. If you can do more, do it.

A Queen move is all about changing the behavior, so yes realistically your $1000+ savings will help guard against the temptation to use credit for an expense that can be covered by the cash that has been saved. For example, if you have a car, you should think about what if that could occur. You may have encountered a flat tire or two at some point (I know I have), and good brand tires are costly; at a minimum of $150.00 or more per tire. Having the funds available in cash will allow you to cover the expense using your savings, versus using credit. Isn't that the whole point? Changing your behavior and adopting this method will help you avoid the pitfall of increasing your debt. All a credit card does is push your debt off for a couple more weeks until the next payment is due and charges you interest. Leveraging credit can be beneficial, but you want to shift your mindset to be able to address the cost directly as opposed to pushing the cost off on a credit card.

The Emergency Fund:

A NY Times 2021 article by Shawn M Carter, *Who Has Enough Cash to Get Through the Coronavirus Crisis?* stated, "Even before Covid-19, many Americans were living check to check, because of the costs of housing and child care, student debt payments, medical bills... Fewer than half of American adults, just 47 percent, say that they have enough emergency funds to cover three months of expenses.."[1]Not surprising, because this virus caught all of us off guard, however, an emergency fund is necessary. *Remember we are all about changing **our** behavior and mindset concerning money.*

Start an emergency fund: I recommend at a minimum to have $1000 in a separate account and then continue to add to it as you can. There are several ways to do this, one way is using a 52 Weeks Savings Plan, it can be as little as $5 or 10/week. I have an amazing plan in my financial workbook that will help track your savings. At the end of the chapter, you can access this for free as a bonus for investing in yourself.

If you have any questions about any of these strategies, do let me know. As a matter of fact, for your support of this project, I will offer you a complimentary session at *discovery.affirmandpursue.com.*

Only scratch where you can reach - Kenyan Proverb

I love this proverb for as simple as it sounds it speaks volumes. Making a budget doesn't have to be a chore. Yes, it will take time to get used to changing your behavior to create it and abide by it, but it is one of the greatest assets to your financial journey. If you use one of the previously mentioned apps or a spreadsheet, you can include the spending limit that you do not want to exceed; this will be your budget. If you are daring enough, push yourself and make an annual budget and then break it down into months. This will help you visualize your plan and manifest your goal.

With the historical data of actual expenses you have, you can calculate the monthly expense of each item in which you have organized your expenses (dividing expenses by the months that have occurred).

Next, you add those specific expenses that you will have during the year (Christmas gifts, car insurance, or trips, for example) to have the annual vision. Once you have what your "normal" expenses are, it is time to take the scissors and see how much and what to cut. Identify which expenses you can consider eliminating; I recommend you do this gradually; one expense at a time and increase it over time.

When I began paying attention and being more intentional about how I spent my money and managed my finances, I didn't hesitate to cut back or eliminate expenses that no longer aligned with my main goal - to get out of debt. For me, the cable was the first thing to go, and then I called AT&T, Nationwide, Fios and asked for lower rates as well.

Don't shy away from reducing certain expenses, it can only help you when you are developing a realistic budget; because now you'll truly see what your budget can afford or not afford to do for you. I love when I have a surplus that just means I get to assign every dollar to another category. And that brings us to the next topic...

Investing Your Savings

Saving money is good, but it won't get you to financial freedom. Knowing where to invest your surplus is even better. Leaving money saved at home is, by far, not the best option. Even so, many people still do this. The important thing is to research the options available in the market and choose the best type of investment for your money to yield a great return.

What does it mean to invest money and how do you make a profit? We hear the phrase "I invested," referring to many aspects of daily life. I invested in real estate. I invested in a person. What do these situations have in common? All of them are looking for an increase in value.

Investing is very often linked to the concept of money: investing money to be able to have more in the future. In the same way, a company can invest money by purchasing a machine to improve and increase its production.

Many people confuse an investment with the action of savings. They are two very distinct concepts. Savings is money you don't want to lose; it is for your rainy day, your expected expenses or long-term assistance should something happen. Investing on the other hand is subject to the risk of loss. It can be real estate, stocks, mutual funds, whatever the diversification but is subject to the risk of loss. If you decide to invest a sum of money, you do it intending to get something in return (hopefully).

The greatest risk you run is to get less from your investment. This can happen if you decide to use your money in situations that you are not familiar with. Not all investments are good investments. Before investing, ask yourself if the investment will meet your financial goal. It is a solid company by reviewing the projections and any other financial reports or information that is available to you. Consider how much time you have available for your investment to return a profit (or gain back to you) and is it feasible for the financial goals you need to meet.

Time is something we can't get back. So should you decide to use the money you have saved and invest it, ensure you seek a qualified expert who can help you weigh the best options depending on what you are looking to do and your risk tolerance. These elements should be considered so you are well informed.

Queen Moves - Research & Invest. Let Your Money Work For You!

Once you have your emergency fund of at least $1k, a debt payoff strategy, have 3-6 months of expenses in savings; now let your money work for you instead of you working for your money. NOTE: This is beyond the 401ks that your employer offers, I am referring to opening up an individual brokerage account and actively selecting growth or dividend stocks, ETFs, mutual funds. I am never one to say just solely invest via your 401k plan at your job because there may be funds that interest you that your employer may not offer AND you may have specific cases for when you want to use your investments ahead of disbursement of your 401k for retirement.

It's important to do your extensive research before you start investing in stocks, real estate, etc.

If you would like and it fits in your budget you can hire a financial expert (advisor) to actively manage your portfolio and ensure that you are investing in the proper companies.

Powerful Reasons Why You Need To Invest:

1. Invest in stocks to grow your money. When done properly, the goal is to double, triple, or even quadruple your initial investment over time.
2. Invest in stocks to save for your retirement. You can't fully rely on social security. You must ensure you and your family will have enough income to retire and live a comfortable lifestyle.
3. Investing in Dividend Stocks to Build Passive Income- Dividend stocks pay you on either a monthly, quarterly, or yearly basis for every stock that you own. This one is my favorite reason to invest. It's all about the dividends Queen!!!

Queen, you have to decide how to create and achieve your investment goals. Where do you want to be?

- Debt-Free?
- 5 or 6 figure months?
- Assets that become your source of income?
- Travel 2-4 times per year?

Whatever it is for you, the foundational elements previously mentioned still apply, but you must also have a strategy in place to meet your investment goals. When you have money invested into the stock market, it is an investment that is at risk of loss. Lastly, I want to ensure you have a full view of your options, not just the ones we normally hear about, that are subject to market fluctuations. I'll explain more in the next chapter.

[2]Shawn M. Carter, "56% of Americans are living paycheck to paycheck — and 43% really need the third stimulus," *Acorns*, March 22, 2021.

Chapter 4: Build Your Assets In A Different Way

My Focus Is Building My Assets, Not My Credit Score
- Yvonne Brown

So far, Queen, you have been informed about the importance of adjusting your mindset which can assist in developing clear and solid financial goals. You have learned how to make Queen moves that can help you identify where you can cut unnecessary spending and crush debt, and you have received helpful tools to begin the process of acquiring and maintaining an emergency fund for those unexpected expenses that would make you reach for your credit card without considering the additional costs. With this information and these steps under your belt, it's time to affirm and pursue wealth.

You have probably heard the saying that **"Money can be a good tool but a cruel master**." As this saying implies, money can be a useful resource when we become better stewards of it. Our ideas of what is and is not possible begin in our minds; this is why I started this book explaining the importance of mindset. Everything begins in the mind, that new venture, building your business, starting a new job, taking a course, etc. You will not know or believe in what is possible for you unless you adopt a mindset of abundance. Why? Because You Are Worthy. Loved. Enough. Do you believe it? There is a scripture that alludes to this very fact:

The plans of the diligent lead to profit as surely as the haste leads to poverty. Proverbs 21:5 (NIV)

Queen, believing in your ability to live in abundance, creates the drive and energy needed to make the moves needed to live abundantly. Money is a tool, a God-given resource that needs to be used effectively on this earth. Once you get clear by reframing your financial perspective, you have moved into a strategic position to build assets in the right manner.

Queen Moves require taking risks; going beyond just hoping for an abundant life, but actualizing the vision by taking action on the basic financial concepts discussed in earlier chapters without being limited to traditional methods of saving and investing (i.e. 401k, IRA, CDs), which are subject to taxes. It implies adding some non-traditional methods, which can grow tax-free.

For years, I spent money with a financial advisor understanding and investing in the traditional approach. It was not without fail, I learned a great deal, but if I can be honest there is so much more that I was not exposed to. In today's society, there are many social platforms (media, podcasts, newspapers, etc., that provide a constant stream of information; new concepts for how to make money. However, most of these resources have some limitations - inflation, taxes, going back into debt, needing a credit score, to name a few. What if there was another way to avoid all of those aforementioned financial pitfalls? There is and it is a strategy that I was introduced to recently and if you will just shift your mindset and lean in, you may find the pot of gold at the end of the rainbow.

I want to introduce you to the concept of using a participating whole life insurance contract as a financial tool. Using this financial tool to supplement your retirement, pay for education, buy a car, a home, simply to cover your financial wants and needs. It is real and it is true and has been around for a very long time and is a key wealth-building strategy for the wealthy and the very banks that you use to save your hard-earned coins or fund your lifestyle.

Let me be very very clear, I am not a licensed agent, I am merely providing information on tools I have used to help me with my financial goals. I believe that when you have access to the right information, you should share it; and it is up to the person to decide if they would like to add it to their financial plan. Dwayne Burnell, the author of *A Path To Financial Peace Of Mind*, mentions key aspects of using participating whole life insurance as a financial vehicle:

> *Participating whole life means the policy pays a dividend to its policy owners because a mutual company is a private company operating solely for the benefit of its participating life policy owners.*
>
> *Not subject to short-term performance demands of the stock market because it is owned by the policy owners.*
>
> *It has a living benefit component so it is possible to borrow against your policy using the cash value as collateral, while your cash value continues to grow even when you take money out.*
>
> *The living benefit is separate from the death benefit provided by the policy.*
>
> *The premiums paid to create a growing asset aka the cash value. Your money is not in the stock market and is working for you with minimal risk*
>
> *Dividends paid to grow tax-deferred and become part of the cash value.*
>
> *You may repay your loan on any schedule you want.*
>
> *Loans you receive are not considered taxable income.*
>
> *Policies are properly designed so that it works for you and your family as a long-term financial tool.*[3]

I have given you a lot here, but to sum it up, with the use of this tool, you will be able to liquidate your assets, use and control your money without penalty or tax. That is powerful in and of itself because the majority of our income goes to inflation, taxes, debt, and big business. The 401k will be subject to taxes once withdrawn and if you need it sooner than the qualified age, a penalty.

Additional benefits to choosing this financial strategy for wealth building include: if for any reason you need to request a loan you don't need to jump through hoops to get your money. It is yours without penalty.

Queen, when you consider your financial goals and the strategy to have assets. Please keep in mind: Liquidity, Tax Advantage, and Flexibility. These three things have been important to me as I look for the types of accounts I save and invest in. As I have become more aware of what is possible, I now know that Queen Moves is not just about creating cash flow, it's about creating wealth. Therefore, it is time I begin to learn and execute like those who are wealthy do.

Understand when you are considering insurance as a financial vehicle, it falls in one of three tax buckets.

1. Tax Now: Money Market, Savings, CDs, Brokerage Accounts, etc.
2. Tax Later: 401k, 403b, TSP Annuities, Traditional IRA
3. Tax Never: Life Insurance, Roth IRA, Municipal Bonds

I don't know about you, but if I can grow my money and take it out later without taxes (see IRS Tax Code:7702), that sounds like something you should consider. However, if you are looking to diversify your assets, you should have your money in each one of these buckets, as the wealthy do, the third option is where you want to begin.

If you are like me and just hearing this new concept for the first time, you are probably thinking WOW!!! Queen, I Know. But this is not a new wealth strategy, it's just not a strategy that has been shared unless you are exposed to the right circles. The very bank that you deposit your money, uses this financial tool and has been using it for a very long time. Why not become a bank? Why not be your own banker?

Remember in chapter 2, subtopic - Cutting The Credit Card and how your interest funds someone else's loan? Well, this is a reason to consider this strategy. Interest is not paid to you. Fund yourself, become the bank, and cut out YOUR bank.

Inflation is an invisible tax. It eats the interest you would've earned. Using this strategy, the money you put into your policy will outperform inflation as uninterrupted compound interest.

I know this may take some time to grasp and I encourage you to do your research and when ready I can connect you to an expert who can assist you further. You can always schedule a complimentary session at ***discovery.affirmandpursue.com*** to learn more.

Empowering you with this information was the main focus for this chapter and I hope I have opened your mind to the possibilities to make Queen Moves, in order to soar in your finances.

> *"You finance everything you buy - you either pay interest to someone else or you give up interest you could have earned otherwise." - R. Nelson Nash*

---

[3]Dwayne Burnell, MBA, A Path To Financial Peace Of Mind, (Bothwell, WA Financial Ball Game Publishing, 2011), pgs.34-35,37-38,40-42,50 .

Chapter 5: Safeguard Your Assets

Peace is costly, but worth the expense (Kenyan Proverb)

Now that you have information on how to make your money work for you and build your wealth, it's time to talk about how to maintain your wealth and grow. As the proverb above indicates, financial peace is costly; it means changing your perspective, sacrificing some wants, learning to identify the difference between a want and a need, and putting in the time. It also implies that the cast is worth it; it's worth it because, with a good perspective and a solid foundation (needs identified, emergency savings, smart ways to invest), you can live abundantly and continue to sustain and build your wealth.

Making money is only half the battle; keeping it safe is the other part. However, if you read financial posts, over 50 percent of the articles are about ways to make money. **Saving money doesn't make big headlines, but it's vital to your long-term success.** With that in mind, I want to talk about some important ways that can help preserve your wealth. There are many avenues that you can leverage to safeguard your wealth and ensure you sustain and protect the wealth you are building. The following are a few of them:

Create an estate plan and establish a will

Find a reputable attorney who specializes in estate planning. There are many reasons to establish a will; some include asset protection, a plan, and a guide to continue your legacy after your death, to provide benefits to your family members, support your favorite cause, prevent your loved ones from ending up in a probate court, and many other things. It is a requirement.

Diversify

Queen, when I say diversify, I mean simply to spread out your investments across a variety of products/assets. This will help you divide your money between more and less risky investments. One way you can consider diversifying is as follows: you can have a percentage of your assets in the stock market, which must be diversified into several different products, such as fixed income, emerging markets, technology stocks, bonds, etc. Also, have a cash percentage to maintain liquidity to take advantage of any opportunity that arises. And if you wish, a percentage of your assets invested in real estate. For example, the wealthy have real estate as part of their portfolio. I learned recently that Edward Johnson (the founder of Fidelity Investments), and Warren Buffett all have real estate as part of their portfolio; and because they own businesses and want to utilize the tax advantages, they have vacation homes in Bermuda. Bermuda is a tax shelter for real estate. Clever! But the main point here is you can diversify into different kinds of real estate, such as industrial buildings, offices, shopping malls, and apartment buildings.

Preserving your money is about keeping it safe. Sometimes this can mean minimizing your tax bills, taking precautions against those who want a piece of what you have worked so hard to build. The goal of preserving money is to have something to retire with and also to be able to leave something for your children and even your grandchildren.

Find a good CPA and listen to them

A good tax advisor will stay on top of the latest changes in tax laws and will find legal ways to minimize your tax bill and tailor it to your specific situation. Just make sure the person you work with is credible and has a good reputation. Bad tax advice or trying to hide government money in foreign accounts is not advisable.

Seek good legal advice

Good legal advice is essential to preserving your wealth. Face it, when you get to the top, you can become the target of envy from others, so you need to protect your assets from predators. Lawyers should also review all business contracts including those between family and friends with whom you are doing business. If there is a dispute, ask for advice before saying or doing something you may regret.

Stick to what has worked for you: don't follow every new investment trend

The problem with the latest money generation trends is that they don't have a track record; there are no success stories. Also, new trends often attract too many people looking to take advantage of the same opportunities. There is nothing wrong with dabbling in something new but look for something that is not so saturated that everyone can't make a profit.

When it comes to significant funds, you shouldn't venture too far out of your comfort zone whether you're investing or expanding your business unless you have a lot of money and risk tolerance for risky investments. Many companies have tried to expand outside their fields, but few have been successful.

Get Good Insurance

This is probably one of the most important tips of all. Many entrepreneurs have insufficient insurance or are not covered at all by certain catastrophes such as earthquakes, hurricanes, strong winds, hail, floods, etc. Find an experienced and reputable insurance broker who can design the policies that best suit you and your investments. I am a huge proponent of a broker because they are not loyal to just one company and will locate the best deal for you.

Psychological Protection

Queen, it is important to understand what I mean by wealth and what it takes to maintain it. Factored into my definition of wealth is peace of mind. Wealth means living a life that is free of financial stressors, being able to see the fruits of the seeds that you have planted, and knowing now, with your new perspective, that what you desire is achievable; you have what it takes to make your dreams a reality. Queen, affirm your desires, hold firm to the vision that you have for yourself because you are in control of making queen moves.

You should know that not everyone thinks like a Queen and therefore will not always be in support of your success. It is important to establish some boundaries with those around you to protect your assets. I'm sure growing up you might have heard the saying " Not everything is for everybody." Be thoughtful and mindful of who you share your perspective and assets with. Work Buddies are just that- work buddies, neighbors are for being neighborly and friends are for friendship. It does not mean you can't share but it does mean you need to ask yourself, how is sharing my perspective and assets going to improve my current financial situation. Sharing should be with a purpose. The saying goes, "Faces we see, hearts we do not know." You should always know what your purpose is in sharing information about yourself and how it will benefit you and the other person. If it does not benefit you in any way, do not share it. This means then, how you carry yourself matters as well.

Protect your peace by protecting your assets. Here are a couple of pointers to help:

Be modest

Queen, learn that being simple and modest is the best practice. What do I mean by this? Just because you have more doesn't mean you have to show out. Remember we are changing our behavior, so we don't fall prey to lifestyle inflation and the glitz and glamour that tends to creep in when we have it all. It's ok to live below your means and still drive the car that is paid off. If you do choose to indulge and buy nice things that is fine too, just don't get sucked back into bad habits, and then you'll have to start all over again. Continue to add assets NOT liabilities to your life. During my financial journey, I have had the same car since 2013, and have no plans to upgrade to a more premium car anytime soon. My car is good on miles and gas and very economical when it is time to take it for service. When that time comes and I choose to upgrade, there is no need to publish my recent purchase for all to see. I am naturally private with such matters, so when you see me you would know before I shout it to the world... LOL.

Be Mindful Of Technology

Although it can be a blessing in some instances if can also be a curse., You will agree it is difficult to live without technology. This still does not release us from using wisdom. We must pay close attention to everything we do. Simply from the web pages we access or by sharing on our social networks, we leave a footprint of our location. Try to use encrypted data and refrain from sharing too much of your life and that of your family on social networks. A little common sense can go a long way.

Queen, take time now to reflect on what has been shared thus far. Write down below how you will change your behavior. What will you begin to implement to ensure your assets and life are guarded so your peace is not compromised?

1.

2.

3.

Show up for you first by realizing you are worth saving, so get rid of all that no longer serves you... You Deserve To Exhale
- Yvonne Brown

Chapter 6: How To Have It All - Income Strategies

From the Words of the legendary investor Warren Buffet "If you don't find a way to make money while you sleep, you will work until you die."

My overall mission is to empower women to become the best version of themselves; this includes becoming financially stable and building wealth so that they can achieve their goals and enjoy the life they deserve. You really can have it all by being a good steward of your money!

As of April 30th, 2020, I submitted my final student loan payment, and it was a wonderful, freeing feeling. I no longer owe American Education Services any more of my hard-earned money. I no longer owe them a dime! When I started accelerating my payments in October of 2019, I had one focus - student debt BE GONE! I felt sick to my stomach knowing how much interest I had already paid up to that date. One of my personal goals is to become debt-free.

In 2013, I was laid off from my job with a great deal of debt. It took me 14 months to find a job. There wasn't a major pandemic, but there is one today called COVID-19. There is an impact on everyone - directly or indirectly. For some of us who still work a 9 to 5, we are faced with low profits, salary cuts, more work, mental exhaustion, and worry.

No one truly knows what the future will hold for this economy. It's time to make moves. You have to have a ***by any legal means necessary*** mentality; the right mindset, a coach, strategies, and tools in place to help you win, and more importantly, so you can have it all.

Using unconventional means to get you to the life you deserve is becoming more common. All along my debt journey, I referred to a database of gigs that I could utilize to bring in extra income. Which has helped me to pay off debt.

One of the simplest and easiest ways is to generate passive income. You can do this by selling a product online. This is a very simple business model: you simply create a website or a sales page, select a product, sell that product from your sales page, and then direct traffic there. It may not start in a passive capacity but if done right can bring in income on autopilot.

This could be an ebook, a webinar course, audio training, a range of different products. The more traffic you can send to your site, the more you will sell. That means you can then start to invest more and more money to increase and scale your business or you can repeat the model with multiple different products.

In the conventional model, selling a product meant one of two things:

- Creating and manufacturing your item
- Buying items in bulk and then selling them off at a lower price point (reselling)
- But some of the other options we are looking at are:
- Affiliate marketing
- Selling your digital product
- Print On Demand (POD)
- Drop-Shipping
- Freelancing

Print on Demand (POD): Print on Demand is simple: you have a product for sale, and as customers order, you place the order with the vendor, and they take care of the rest. You don't need inventory, you don't ship anything, and can start with little to no money. The company that you work with does the heavy lifting for you. If you find the right niche, the sky's the limit with the POD model.

Digital Products: Everyone can create a digital product. It involves selling directly through the internet. You can build a whole business off of digital products. It can be an eBook, planner, pdfs, or a masterclass. No matter what your niche is. You can create digital products around your skills, passion, or expertise. There's no shipping involved and allows you to make money 24/7. Digital Products can be 100% fully automated. Bonus: It's a furlough, COVID, and recession-proof!! For example, once you've made *one* eBook, you can sell it an infinite number of times and through an automated process with no need to handle anything personally.

This also gives you complete freedom over what you sell specifically and how you want to market and price it. Just keep in mind that you're going to have to create the product yourself, and that means you'll need to invest a little extra time upfront or hire someone to create it for you.

Dropshipping: Another option is dropshipping. This is essentially somewhere between selling your physical product and selling an affiliate product.

A dropshipping company is any company that will allow you to sell their products and then pass that sale on to them. They will then pay you a cut (typically more than regular affiliate commission for digital products – they essentially act as wholesalers, which means 50/50) and will handle everything from the packaging to the fulfillment to any complaints they may have from their customers.

The best part? A lot of dropshipping companies are happy to be "white label." This means that they operate like silent partners, never promoting their brand to your end-user. You can thereby sell your product online and create the impression that you are working as a regular online store. The company will deliver the product on your behalf, but it will look as though it has come from you.

Better yet, some of these companies will even go so far as to allow you to tweak the product or redesign it. That means that you can have your logo on it or even create something entirely new from scratch. A perfect example of this might be selling a supplement: here, the dropshipping company will let you choose the formulation and will let you put your brand on the product. From there, you can then sell the product to your audience and they will send it out each time you pass the sale on to them. They'll never know that you didn't create it in your very own factory.

In short, this is the perfect way to have your cake and eat it too! Find dropshipping companies through sites like Alibaba.com or use Google and search for "White Label Dropshipping" in your chosen industry.

Freelancing: Very, very popular. Essentially, you're offering yourself/skills out for hire. A graphic designer, virtual assistant, content creator, or social media manager. If you are between jobs or need extra money and have an in-demand skill set, this is a great way to bring in additional income. There are sites where you can set up your profile via Upwork.com, Guru.com, and Fiverr.com, just to name a few. Get hired, do good work, and get referrals and repeat clients.

Affiliate Marketing: This is great if you want to get started making money and you have no product at all. Being an affiliate of someone else's products means you promote their product and customer purchase using your affiliate link where you get a percentage of that sale. You're like an extended marketing team aka brand ambassador for any company no matter the niche. The key with affiliate marketing is to start with brands you know and love and get paid!

Additionally, I wanted to share with you a few income strategies I have used:

- Purged my closets and sold items to consignment shops
- Print on Demand: Started a side hustle selling t-shirts and inspirational items

- Became a landlord, extra cash flow from rental applied to debt
- Digital Products: Created and sold eBooks, planners, courses
- Became an affiliate of brands I know and trust

Queen, the point of this section truly paints multiple ways to make money and some can be passive. You see, passive income is career insurance. Creating the right product at the right price point can help you earn that additional money you need to keep your peace, to keep earning 'sleep coins' so there is less dependency on earned income, to pay off the debt, and to build assets. You see, if you want something different, you have to put in the work to get it and push yourself out of your comfort zone.

[4]"As long as your money is caught up at the mall; in exchanging places with depreciating cars; and keeping company with Mastercard, Visa, and Discover, and consumer debt, it will never make it to the sandboxes of the seven figure club." - LaShawne Holland

---

[4] LaShawne Holland, Born To Multiply, (Bloomington, IN Author House, 2019), pg. 137 .

Chapter 7: Key Steps To Creating A Profitable Side Hustle

Affirm: *I am capable of overcoming any money obstacles that stand in my way.*

Queen, I know I have provided a great deal of valuable information up to this point and honestly, I thought about ending the book at step 6 (chapter 6), but I couldn't leave this chapter out. Reading this book alone has provided the coaching you need to get started with soaring in your finances, but this chapter will help you to implement starting a side hustle. If we never meet or get the chance to work together, this will get you started.

I wish I had this knowledge before receiving the pink slip in 2013, I would have paused and said there is something to this and I need to at least consider it, but I didn't have anyone pushing me, coaching me, or sending me details of the how. I believe in giving people the right information, so they can make the choice that is right for their finances.

As I mentioned in the last chapter, no one truly knows what the future will hold for this economy. You have to have a ***by any means necessary*** mentality (legal way of course); the right mindset, a coach, strategies, and tools in place to help you win, and more importantly, so you can have it all.

'All' is relative and can mean: all your peace, all your money returning interest to you and not a lender, all your children's savings fully funded, traveling around the world, building a real estate empire. Whatever ALL means for you, state it here.

DECLARE: I want to win in this money game, so I can have All

____________________________.

I do hope you will use the God-given resource, money, to enlarge your financial landscape, your kingdom and not remain complacent. Start an additional income stream, using the following steps below to begin charting a plan today. Guess what? Rome wasn't built in one day and nothing is perfect the first time you do it. But don't give up, fail fast and rebound and learn from your mistakes, because MISTAKES MAKE MASTERS.

SAY IT: MISTAKES MAKE MASTERS

Now that we know that we will perfect as we go and become masters of our successes, let's get started:

Map Out Your Hustle Idea And Strategy

A key component for success in your side hustle is having a plan. As often said, failing to plan is planning to fail and that applies here 100%. You need a solid strategy for your side hustle. Better than anyone else, you know your strengths and weaknesses, so you have a good chance to use your strength and eliminate weaknesses. Don't be afraid to ask for help in areas of weakness from family and friends. Ask them to help you come up with a strategy for your side hustle. As for yourself, write out everything you can think of and edit them later. Don't make the mistake of editing while writing as this slows the creative process down. Ensure you cannot think of any other idea before you start going through the list.

Lists vs Mind Maps:

A linear list or mind maps are great tools to organize your ideas. Both are cool, but one is better at representing your ideas and compacting them on one page. A linear list is mostly long, discouraging, and overwhelming to go through and doesn't show you if any of your previous ideas are related to a present one.

A mind map, on the other hand, makes everything concise and organized. It gives you a bird's eye view of your ideas and helps to bring everything to the point. Mind maps are great for your planning process much more than a list. There are lots of great mind map tools out there like Bubble and Mindomo. Their free versions allow you to create up to 3 mind maps.

Your Edge:

One thing to keep in mind as you create your strategy is your competitive advantage. That is your edge. What is your unique selling proposition? How are you different from all your competitors? What do you have that they don't?

Your answer to these questions is what constitutes your edge and things you should use when reaching out to potential clients. They are quite difficult to answer, but once you do, it puts you at an advantage so when clients ask you, you know what you are going to say. The fact that you can answer them will show any potential client that you have paid your dues and will deliver.

People won't believe that you are better than the competition simply because you said so. You need to think outside of the box and give a solid reason with proof that you are who you say you are.

Branding Your Side Hustle:

Branding is another thing to consider and build as you go along. Most women think of this as unnecessary because they side hustlers and don't need any of these things. This is wrong.

To succeed with your side hustle, you may need to brand yourself. Becoming a brand positions you as an authority figure, thereby making clients trust in your ability to deliver. If your branding is right, you won't need to do much marketing as your brand speaks volumes for you. For your big picture, branding might be the secret ingredient you need.

It's All About The Details:

Due to the number of things you have to do and figure out, you might be thinking you can do away with some things and try to work on them when they pop up on your journey. As alluring as that sounds, don't make this mistake.

Ideally, you want to reduce challenges and setbacks as much as possible. This is why planning is of great necessity. You are reading this guide to learn how to put yourself on the right path to success, right? Well, to succeed, you have to plan things and look deeply into the details.

You want to be proactive, not reactive. As the saying goes, prevention is better than cure so it's better you prevent things from happening instead of reacting to them.

Analyze And Validate Your New Hustle Data

The thought of quitting your job is a scary one for a lot of women being that it's a radical move and most women who have tried it failed. However, this shouldn't be so. With a properly planned strategy, you can quit your day job and transition smoothly to your side hustle. To minimize failure and maximize your success, you need to take your time to analyze and validate your side hustle data. This will help you see which hustles are worth your time and which ones should be left to burn.

Depending on the hustle you chose, you might have to spend money on validating and analyzing its profitability. This might mean borrowing some tools and resources to properly research. That said, keep your spending to a minimum as you don't want to go buying things you might not need.

Analyze Your Competitors:

What are your competitors doing? How are they marketing their services and to whom are they marketing? What can you do better? How can you beat them at their game even if they have been there before you?

Ask yourself, *"If I were a customer, would I buy my products? Would I rather buy from the competition and why would I? Why and why not?"* The answers to these questions will let you know where you stand.

Go where your competitors are and do what they are doing. If they are posting on social media, do the same. Make findings of what type of content their followers love and engage with the most. Afterward, create a list of what you will do and how you can do better.

The main purpose of this analysis is to know whether you stand a chance in the hustle you've chosen. It will be a total waste of time to compete in a business you don't stand a chance in. Get feedback from your audience.

It doesn't make sense to put resources into something only for those you are creating it for to not want it. You want to get your business in front of the audience that needs it and would want to do business.

To make sure your target audience will buy what you are selling, you need feedback from those who fit your target demographics. Let's say that your target market is small business owners in California with one or two employees. You can try looking for those who fit that profile and post questions on social media and several forums.

Tender your offer and allow them to comment if they like what you do. If yes, why do they like it? If not, why don't they like it? Detailed answers will help you improve on things you should improve on rather than working blindly. Don't forget to thank them for their time and attention.

Do A Soft Launch:

Since you are still validating your idea, it will be good not to dive in completely. This means if you are selling a physical product, you shouldn't jump into creating hundreds while you are still validating your data.

You will have wasted resources and efforts on something your target audience doesn't want if nobody buys it. This applies especially to E-Commerce as you want to be sure there is demand for your product.

If your test turns out successful, that means you have a gold mine in your hands. If it doesn't, that simply means you should go back to the drawing board; it doesn't mean you've failed. You are only looking for a profitable and suitable side hustle.

Set Realistic Goals And Timeline With Your Hustle

Like the name says, you think of your side hustle as an afterthought, which means it's not your full-time job. You're working at your hustle on days when you don't go to your office work or even before/after you go to work. Your schedule will rely upon you and how busy you are at the workplace. When you're starting your hustle, you should be reasonable with your goals. Without a doubt, you may think your hustle has genuine potential, and you want it to grow to acquire 10 times your income or something to that effect. However, do you think you have a chance to commit to your business? Think about this carefully or you'll wind up disillusioning yourself.

Goal Setting:

You can focus on aspiring and grandiose goals. You can likewise focus on amazingly simple goals or the other hand, focus on the widely appealing goals: not very hard and not very simple. When you focus on ambitious goals, you may stress yourself to death. You'll take on more work than you can manage, you'll miss deadlines, have customers griping about your low-quality work, and so on. You don't need that. When you force yourself to accomplish something you just can't do, you're killing yourself.

At the furthest edge of the spectrum, if you focus on goals that are excessively simple for you, then you may end up procrastinating. You'll figure, "I can do that in one day. I'll do it tomorrow. I'll simply go play on my PC today." So, you end up not busy and waste a ton of time.

The right goals would be something that will push you or challenge you to use your time carefully. You're not going to wait, and simultaneously, you're not going to drive yourself up the wall. Along these lines, you're productive, and you eventually bring yourself closer to your goals.

Your Goal Timelines:

There are three distinct timelines for goals. With regards to your side hustles, you can set short-term goals, long-term goals, or life goals. For short-term goals, consider what you want to accomplish with your side hustle in the coming weeks or months. Ask yourself the amount you need to acquire in the following month or something along that line, and how you intend to accomplish that goal. Having a daily, weekly, and monthly plan or agenda would also be useful. It will help keep you on target and ensure you stick to exactly what you've planned.

For your long-term goals, consider where you need your side hustle to be in say, one to five years. Do you think you'll be working solo? Or do you envision that your business will have grown and you'll have a team? Or do you think you'll be working at your day job?

For your life goals, this is THE main goal. What is the aim of your side hustle? Where do you see yourself in the future? The CEO will see your side hustle become a worldwide phenomenon. Whatever your life's purpose might be, ensure your short-term and long-term goals line up with it.

Constantly Reexamine Your Goals:

Your goals aren't unchangeable. After some time, you may understand that a few of your goals may not be practical. Along these lines, you have to adjust and modify needs. There's no compelling reason to worry if you don't accomplish your goals as planned. Essentially, rethink your goals and attempt to think of something more attainable.

For instance, if you find that one of your goals was excessively difficult or too convoluted to even think about achieving inside the time period you picked, then maybe you might need to change the time span or scrap that goal completely. Nobody's going to reprimand you. If you have to change your goals, then do so. You're most likely only a one-man show now in your side hustle. Don't be so difficult on yourself.

Getting excited about the process and the journey is important. You have a major goal you need to accomplish someday. You're not going to have the option to do that if you scrutinize yourself each time you make a mistake. Learn from your missteps and your failures. It's the only way you will grow as a business person and as an individual.

Create And Follow A Strict Side Hustle Schedule

How free are you on a workday? Furthermore, how free are you on your days off? How long do you need for your schedules? For rest? For family time? There are a lot of reasons why you have to make and follow an exacting side hustle plan. For one, you've just got 24 hours in a day. That is fixed, non-debatable. In any case, you must include your day job, your side hustle, and everything else inside this time span.

If you would prefer not to die young, then you have to take measures not to stretch yourself to death. You have to manage your body. You have to evaluate your physical, mental, and emotional health every once in a while. The purpose behind this is that if you become ill, then you can't work. It's as straightforward as that.

Plan Your Day:

Arranging your schedule every day will help guarantee you avoid taking on beyond what you can practically manage. You can, unfortunately, do a limited amount of work in one day. For instance, if you have a blog as a side hustle, then plan out what number of words you ought to compose every day. If that doesn't work for you, then consider what number of posts you can reasonably compose and upload in seven days.

Recall that consistency is vital to prevail in nearly anything in everyday life, and it's particularly significant for side hustles! Since you are your own boss, you have to structure your day so you don't procrastinate and do things you shouldn't do!

Expand Your Time:

Carefully following your schedule will help amplify your time. You do need your side hustle to be beneficial, isn't that so? Along these lines, find a way to do errands that will help boost your time and your productivity. Have a framework set up or a procedure that will assist you with getting from servicing a customer to submitting their projects in the most productive manner conceivable.

You may begin with a model of your framework (let's call it framework A). However, you'll find it's not as successful as framework B. If this happens, then you have to make alterations. You have to take the necessary steps to be as productive as could be expected under the circumstances.

You can't simply say you'll stay with framework A because that is what you thought of first or that is what's written on your whiteboard or any place. Don't be hesitant to change plans. You must take the necessary steps to maximize your time.

Focus on One Thing At A Time:

Multitasking is great, but as a rule, it can slow you down. It's so natural to lose focus when you perform multiple tasks. It's anything but difficult to get overpowered by the various things you have to do. For instance, suppose you're doing some customer work, sitting in front of the TV, and looking at social media simultaneously. You're most likely not going to accomplish much. When it's time to work on your side hustle, turn off the distractions.

Put your telephone on quiet mode if it won't be used for your side work. Turn off the TV. Find a way to ensure you focus on what you're working on. Trust me, you will complete such a large number of things when you've expelled the distractions (they're called distractions as they should be!). You may even have the option to complete your assignments before the delivery day. When you do this, then you can compensate yourself by watching some TV until it's time to work on the next item on your priorities for the day.

Remember to Reward Yourself:

There's nothing as satisfying as having to check off things on your plan for the day. When you're on a schedule, it's occasionally difficult to consider compensating yourself when your booked vacation is five days away. The thing is, you don't have to spend extravagantly, but don't avoid rewarding yourself either.

For example, if you have done everything on your agenda for the day, then you can remunerate yourself with an additional hour watching the TV or on the other hand, order your preferred takeout food so you can make TV time significantly more pleasant. If you have met your expectations for the week, then reward yourself with a rental to watch the most recent blockbuster film. Discipline and commitment are key to carefully follow a schedule, especially for a side hustle. If you succeed, then you surely merit whatever prize you have planned.

Focus On What Generates Revenue:

However much as could be expected, you need to produce some income each time you work on your side hustle. Therefore, you must make sense of how you can smooth out your procedures and your frameworks to think of the most productive "formula." As you know, not all side hustles are made equivalent. Some side hustles are direct while some are more convoluted and require intensive planning. If you're occupied with a "less difficult" side hustle, then producing income is as basic as offering your support to your neighbors.

Now with regards to producing incomes for more complex side hustles, you would need to concentrate your time on exercises that make you cash. Here are a few thoughts:

Focus On Your Target Audience:

Before you began your side hustle, you should have had a thought of who your optimal customers and clients are. Say, for example, you need to mentor kids. Before you go around marketing your business, you should recognize what sort of subjects you're going to teach, what evaluation levels you're going to deal with, and so forth.

If you're caring for children, you may need to just think about children of particular ages. In case you're not open to being alone with a small child, then that is fine. You can simply decide to watch four years of age or older. Generally, making a buyer persona of your intended interest group is useful. It's simpler for you to make offers that they'll find fascinating. For example, if you have an outsourcing business, you'd likely publicize your business on different social media channels (you have to invest both energy and cash to do this). If your focus is on the wrong audience, then you're not going to get many conversions. However, if your ads and focus are on the right group who will profit by purchasing your items, then you may rake in tons of cash!

In this way, that is what you need to happen. You need to boost your ROI. The most ideal approach to do that is by placing your ads and your brand before the right crowd. If you don't, then your cash is going to go down the drain.

Focus on Generating and Nurturing Leads:

We can't downplay the significance of lead generation. Without a pipeline loaded with leads, you'll be battling to remain above water. Without great leads, how are you going to create income for your side hustle?

A great marketing methodology will assist you with topping off your pipeline with quality leads. Yet, you can't simply leave it at that. Rather, you need to sustain your leads, so they inevitably become paying customers. Lead generation can be done physically or automated. For manual lead generation, you can request referrals from your current system like your friends and even your customers. You can try offering a discount to any individual who sends some new clients your way.

Computerized lead generation, is mostly used by online organizations. You can set up a landing page with an extremely luring offer. When individuals download or look at your offer, they enter their contact details on the page. All you need to do then is get in touch with them, then make a valiant effort to convert them into paying customers.

Focus on Customer Service

A few women downplay customer service. They believe there's no cash to be had in giving great customer service. Though, this isn't evident, it can kill your side hustle completely!

Unsatisfied customers can easily go on the web and post about their terrible experience with your business. Word can immediately spread about you. Individuals who haven't known about you will Google you. When they read your negative audits, they will go somewhere else. They're not going to risk their cash with you. However, if you treat your clients right and do what you say you will, then they'll be happy campers. They'll be faithful to your brand, become repeat clients, and the best part is that they'll tell their friends about you. As you probably are aware, word of mouth is one of the best types of marketing. Soon, you'll have a larger number of leads in your business pipeline than you can manage.

Do the best you can until you know better. Then when you know better, do better. - Maya Angelou

Conclusion

Well, Queen, we are at the end of our journey together. At this point, I hope you have received enough information and insight to help you take flight and soar. When I thought about writing this book, I honestly didn't know what to say or even what to title it. It went through several name changes and I am glad I settled on a simplistic title. Queen Moves is all about taking your rightful position in the world of finance; and that can only happen with the right mindset, the right coach, and the right strategies.

I am all about helping Queens understand the basics of financial matters. For your support of this project, I will offer you a complimentary session at discovery.affirmandpursue.com designed to help you get on the path for money matter success.

You see, even in the game of chess, the Queen is the most powerful on the board. Queen, you're already built with a superpower to withstand any self-limiting beliefs that say you are not worthy of having it all. You Are. You Can. You Will.

Affirm: *Abundance is coming, I deserve and accept it*

You see when you operate in excellence and handle the God-given resource, money effectively, you join others who handle personal finances well and act with caution, and know when to make intentional decisions with your money. Queen Moves is about saving yourself from financial ruin and doing the things now however mundane, however tedious, boring whatever you want to call it so that you can develop healthy habits. It's all about changing your behavior so you can enlarge your territory, using the resource - money, that God supplies.

Queen Moves is all about aligning yourself with those who understand we are not meant to live in debt, "not be a slave to the lender", but be responsible stewards of our money and control our spending, save our coins using traditional or not so traditional means. Queen Moves is all about money management - not obsessing about more money. Queen Moves is all about immersing yourself in wealth-building strategies that you may not have known or been exposed to and taking a step forward to do the research and take action.

Above all, Queen Moves is understanding that solely depending on earned income will not get you to your desired financial state. You must create additional income streams, I recommend those that are passive. Queen, You Deserve To Exhale. That is what Queen Moves is truly all about. Stop dwelling in defeat, in past money mistakes, and take the information that is given and begin anew. Queen, it begins with you taking the first step. It will be uneasy, different, hard, but you were created to seize this moment because you know WHO you are and WHOSE you are - A Daughter Of The Most High.

Create A Wealthy Mindset, Affirm Your Desires, Listen To God Only, Manifest Everything You Desire - Yvonne Brown

About the Author

Yvonne Brown, a native of Philadelphia, Pennsylvania is an international best selling author, speaker, and financial coach and takes a ***crush debt by any legal means necessary*** stance when it comes to freeing women from the burden of debt. After losing her job unexpectedly in 2013 and going without employment for a long period of time. She vowed to never make her job her source but use the tool of money as a resource, in order to set herself up financially and never be at the mercy of a job or government. Since then, she has crushed over $70,000 in debt, paying off her personal loan most recently. Establishing good money habits has saved her over and over! Yvonne is committed to helping women know that past money mistakes will not define who they are because **#mistakesmakesmasters**; and that it is not too late to rewrite their financial narrative. Her **#notme** campaign is paramount to getting Queens to exhale and not be saddled with the multitude of costs (health,financial,relationships,etc.)that can become a negative factor, when you do not have a sound financial strategy. She believes that with the right mindset, the right coach, and blueprint, conquering your financial goals is possible.

"Do the best you can until you know better, and when you know better do better." - Maya Angelou

Connect with her at wwwyvonnebrownexhales.com

@YVONNEBROWNEXHALES

Check Out Additional Books By Yvonne Brown

Money Matters For Side Hustles

12 Step Guide To Starting A Side Hustle

Change your mindset, change your attitude, and release anything that may be holding you back from the possibilities of a lucrative side business. There are so many ideas that can be fruitful, if you'll take the time and explore them. Take action. You'll never know unless you try. What if that one idea acted upon truly propels you into a millionaire? Think about it for a moment. With everything that is going on currently, your story can have a glorious ending. Now is the time to seize the opportunity for greater. It's time to soar!

For more information and to purchase a copy visit
www.yvonnebrownexhales.com

Girl On Fire: Fireproof

Journey with Yvonne Brown and 13 other Trailblazers, Women of Faith, Movers & Shakers who are blazing a TRAIL all over the GLOBE with their Gifts, Talents, Wisdom, & Profound Insights.

Learn how these POWERHOUSE Women battled against the odds, fought against the obstacles of life, and went through the Fire....but came out SMOKELESS.

To purchase contact us at www.yvonnebrownexhales.com

The Evolution Effect

The Evolution Effect is a compilation of 20 stories of individuals who have taken a risk and a leap of faith in themselves. Individuals who are building a legacy and have made drastic changes in their life. We are sharing their stories to help others to face their own traumas, challenges, and overcome adversities. With our collection of stories, we focused on depression, domestic violence, divorce, mental and physical health challenges, sexual assault, childhood traumas. The sole purpose was to work together to share their stories and create a powerful book to impact and inspire millions of lives.

To purchase, contact us at www.yvonnebrownexhales.com

Our Truth Is Not A Lie

”Our Truth Is Not A Lie” is an audio and e-book with 18 compelling stories about the black and brown experience. There are often times our experiences are suppressed and unaddressed. When we share our truths it is either disregarded or minimized. Our Truth is Not A Lie and you will hear us loud and clear. Our voices, visions, and black are ALL powerful and beautiful. We deserve more than matter. We have all worked extremely hard to change the narrative and build a legacy. Listen to our stories.

To purchase contact us at www.yvonnebrownexhales.com

Affirm And Pursue Academy Resources

By Yvonne Brown

Queen Love Thyself! Affirmation Journal And Planner

Made with purity and grace. Strength and love. Deliver positive affirmations into your mind, never miss loving you!

How To Pay Off Thousands In Student Loan Debt Masterclass

Let me show you the strategies I used to pay off my $25K student balance in 7 months.

Budget Mastery: Keys To Budget Like A Beast

It's time to Prepare, Plan And Pursue. It's time to check your Passive Income Status. This class will do just that and more.

30 SIDE HUSTLES YOU CAN START TODAY WITH LITTLE TO NO MONEY!

For additional complimentary bonuses: Download your monthly budget workbook at Affirm & Pursue: Financial Workbook. Use Coupon Code: FREE

Made in United States
Orlando, FL
04 November 2026

90201274R00059